OBJECTIVE APPLICATIONAL ORGANIC CHEMISTRY

MITHLESH CHOUDHARY

ISBN 979-888503764-8

TO MY MOTHER

"Mrs. BEENA CHOUDHARY"

for raising me to believe that, "utilize your present time wisely, it will pay you something unique in future..!"

Contents

Foreword

I, Mithlesh Choudhary, Forwarding this book to those students and aspirants who seek objective multiple choice questions of organic chemistry. I am writing this book because many of the school-going students and competitive candidates learn the theoretical portion of the subject but never practice objective questions, which are equally essential for examinations. Hence, this is my small initiative for those students who want to learn something in a unique and creative way.

I hope the aspirant/students will enjoy this book and my content.

This series will continue in future as well, so keep in touch with me.

The Author

Preface

I have decided to design this book because I wanted to share what I learned from this stunning subject in a unique way and what is the actual essentiality behind organic chemistry. I also wanted to tell everyone and chemistry students, objective questions are very important for the understanding of organic chemistry topics.

I would recommend this book to all the chemistry aspirants and all the competitive candidates to read this book and know the Facts and necessity of all the MCQs.

Practice and Enjoy...!

Mithlesh Choudhary

Acknowledgements

In preparing "Objective Applicational Organic Chemistry" I wish to acknowledge my indebtedness to the wholehearted and vast motivation of my all enthusiastic friends - ABHISHEK, KULDEEP, LAXMAN, DEEPAK, NARESH, AMIT, KRITIKA, SHIVANI, SONU, GOPAL, BHAGWATI, MANISHA.... and all my well-wishing family people.

Sincerest thanks are also due to the person with high integrity and kindness, AYUSH, who constantly supported me in very harsh situations.

Mithlesh Choudhary

Prologue

Organic chemistry is a branch of chemistry that studies the structure, properties and reactions of organic compounds, which contain carbon in covalent bonding. Study of structure determines their structural formula. Study of properties includes physical and chemical properties, and evaluation of chemical reactivity to understand their behavior. The study of organic reactions includes the chemical synthesis of natural products, drugs, and polymers, and study of individual organic molecules in the laboratory and via theoretical (in silico) study.

The range of chemicals studied in organic chemistry includes hydrocarbons (compounds containing only carbon and hydrogen) as well as compounds based on carbon, but also containing other elements, especially oxygen, nitrogen, sulfur, phosphorus (included in many biochemicals) and the halogens. Organometallic chemistry is the study of compounds containing carbon–metal bonds.

In addition, contemporary research focuses on organic chemistry involving other organometallics including the lanthanides, but especially the transition metals zinc, copper, palladium, nickel, cobalt, titanium and chromium.

Organic compounds form the basis of all earthly life and constitute the majority of known chemicals. The bonding patterns of carbon, with its valence of four—formal single, double, and triple bonds, plus structures with delocalized electrons—make the array of organic compounds structurally diverse, and their range of applications enormous. They form the basis of, or are constituents of, many commercial products including pharmaceuticals; petrochemicals and agrichemicals, and products made from them including lubricants, solvents; plastics; fuels and explosives. The study of organic chemistry overlaps organometallic chemistry and biochemistry, but also with medicinal chemistry, polymer chemistry, and materials science.

Mithlesh Choudhary

CHAPTER ONE

OBJECTIVE QUESTIONS (1 TO 450)

1. Which of the following is not a characteristic of organic compounds?
(*a*) They usually have low melting points.
(*b*) They usually are only slightly soluble or insoluble in water.
(*c*) If water soluble they seldom conduct an electric current.
(*d*) Bonds which bind the atoms together are nearly always ionic.
Answer. (*d*)
2. The element least likely to be found in an organic compound is
(*a*) oxygen
(*b*) sulfur
(*c*) nitrogen
(*d*) silicon
Answer. (*d*)
3. One of the major sources of organic compounds is
(*a*) Natural gas
(*b*) Fermentation
(*c*) Sea water
(*d*) Atmosphere
Answer. (*a*)
4. Catenation is a property of the carbon atom which describes its ability to
(*a*) bond with other carbon atoms
(*b*) form double and triple bonds
(*c*) exist in plant and animal form
(*d*) form bonds in its ground state
Answer. (*a*)
5. In stable organic compounds, carbon will always form
(*a*) 2 bonds
(*b*) 4 bonds
(*c*) 3 bonds
(*d*) 5 bonds
Answer. (*b*)
6. Carbon-carbon double bonds consist of :

(*a*) one σ bond, one π bond
(*b*) two σ bonds, one π bond
(*c*) one σ bond, two π bonds
(*d*) two σ bonds, two π bonds
Answer. (*a*)
7. Acetylene has a total of :
(*a*) one σ bond, two π bonds
(*b*) two σ bonds, four π bonds
(*c*) three σ bonds, two π bonds
(*d*) one σ bond, four π bonds
Answer. (*c*)
8. In propene there are
(*a*) eight σ bonds and one π bond
(*b*) seven σ bonds and two π bonds
(*c*) six σ bonds and three π bonds
(*d*) nine σ bonds
Answer. (*a*)
9. In propyne there are
(*a*) six σ bonds and two π bonds
(*b*) seven σ bonds and one π bond
(*c*) six σ bonds and one π bond
(*d*) eight σ bonds
Answer. (*a*)
10. 1-Buten-3-yne has
(*a*) six σ and four π bonds
(*b*) seven σ and three π bonds
(*c*) eight σ and two π bonds
(*d*) nine σ and one π bond
Answer. (*b*)
11. Compound in which carbons use only sp^3 hybrid orbitals for bond formation is
(*a*) $CH_3CH_2CH_3$
(*b*) $CH_3C{\equiv}CH$
(*c*) $CH_3CH{=}CH_2$
(*d*) $CH_2{=}CH{-}CH{=}CH_2$
Answer. (*a*)

12. Compound in which carbon uses *sp*³ hybrid orbitals for bond formation is

(*a*) $H-\overset{\overset{O}{\|}}{C}-H$

(*b*) $H_2N-\overset{\overset{O}{\|}}{C}-NH_2$

(*c*) $H-\overset{\overset{O}{\|}}{C}-OH$

(*d*) $(CH_3)_3COH$

Answer. (*d*)

13. When the carbon atom is sp^2 hybridized in a compound, it is bonded to

(*a*) 2 other atoms

(*b*) 4 other atoms

(*c*) 3 other atoms

(*d*) 5 other atoms

Answer. (*c*)

14. Compound in which carbons use only *sp*2 hybrid orbitals for bond formation is

(*a*) 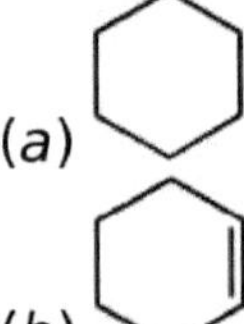

(*b*)

(*c*) $CH_2=CH-CH=CH_2$

(*d*) $CH_3CH=C=CH_2$

Answer. (*c*)

15. Which of the following is a planar molecule?

(*a*) Formaldehyde

(*b*) Acetone

(*c*) Formic acid

(*d*) Acetic acid

Answer. (*a*)

16. What is bond angle between the hybrid orbitals in methane?

(*a*) 180°
(*b*) 120°
(*c*) 109.5°
(*d*) 115.5°
Answer. (*c*)
17. The H–C–C bond angle in ethane is
(*a*) 60°
(*b*) 109.5°
(*c*) 120°
(*d*) 118°28′
Answer. (*b*)
18. The H–C–H bond angle in ethylene is
(*a*) 60°
(*b*) 120°
(*c*) 90°
(*d*) 180°
Answer. (*b*)
19. What is the bond length of a carbon-carbon double bond?
(*a*) 1.20 Å
(*b*) 1.34 Å
(*c*) 1.54 Å
(*d*) 1.68 Å
Answer. (*b*)
20. The carbon-carbon bond lengths in rank of increasing bond length is :
(*a*) triple, double, single
(*b*) single, double, triple
(*c*) single, triple, double
(*d*) triple, single, double
Answer. (*a*)
21. Which of the following is the correct order of bond lengths :
(*a*) C–C < C=C < C≡C
(*b*) C–C > C≡C > C=C
(*c*) C≡C > C–C > C=C

(*d*) C≡C < C–C > C=C
Answer. (*a*)
22. Which of the following hydrocarbons has the shortest C–C bond length?
(*a*) $CH_2=CH_2$
(*b*) CH_3CH_3
(*c*) $HC\equiv CH$
(*d*) 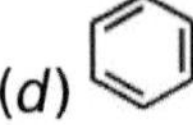
Answer. (*c*)
23. The carbon-carbon bond length is maximum in
(*a*) $CH_2=CH_2$
(*b*) CH_3CH_3
(*c*) $HC\equiv CH$
(*d*) 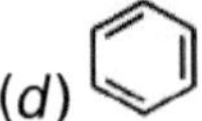
Answer. (*b*)
24. What is the hybridization of the carbon atoms numbered 1 and 2 respectively in the following structure?

$$C_6H_5-CH=\underset{1}{CH}-\underset{2}{C}\equiv CH$$

(*a*) *sp*^{3}, *sp*^{2}
(*b*) *sp*^{2}, *sp*^{2}
(*c*) *sp*, *sp*
(*d*) *sp*^{2}, *sp*
Answer. (*d*)
25. How many atoms are attached to an atom having a *sp* hybridization?
(*a*) 0
(*b*) 1
(*c*) 2
(*d*) 3
Answer. (*c*)
26. Which statement is true?
(*a*) Resonance hybrids are inherently unstable.

(*b*) Resonance hybrids are more stable than any individual resonance form.
(*c*) Resonance hybrids are averages of all resonance forms resembling the less stable forms.
(*d*) Resonance hybrids are averages of all resonance forms resembling the more stable forms.
Answer. (*d*)
27. Resonance structures of a molecule have
(*a*) same arrangement of atoms
(*b*) different arrangement of atoms
(*c*) same number of paired electrons
(*d*) different number of paired electrons
Answer. (*a*) and (*c*)
28. Which of the following compounds have planar molecules?
(*a*) ethyl alcohol
(*b*) formaldehyde
(*c*) diethyl ether
(*d*) 1,3-butadiene
Answer. (*b*) and (*d*)
29. Which of the following compounds will show dipole moment?
(*a*) *cis*-1,2-dichloroethylene
(*b*) *o*-dichlorobenzene
(*c*) *trans*-1,2-dichloroethylene
(*d*) *p*-dichlorobenzene
Answer. (*a*) and (*b*)
30. Which molecule has a nonzero dipole moment?
(*a*) Cl_2
(*b*) CO_2
(*c*) CCl_4
(*d*) $CHCl_3$
Answer. (*d*)
31. Which of the following compounds have lowest dipole moment?
(*a*) carbon tetrachloride

(*b*) chloromethane
(*c*) dichloromethane
(*d*) chloroform
Answer. (*a*)
32. Which molecule has the greatest dipole moment
(*a*) CH_3Cl
(*b*) CH_3Br
(*c*) CH_3F
(*d*) CH_3I
Answer. (*c*)
33. Which of the following compounds have highest dipole moment?
(*a*) dichloromethane
(*b*) chloroform
(*c*) chloromethane
(*d*) carbon tetrachloride
Answer. (*a*)
34. Homolytic fission of C–C bond leads to the formation of :
(*a*) Free radicals
(*b*) Carbonium ions
(*c*) Carbanions
(*d*) None of these
Answer. (*a*)
35. Homolytic fission of covalent bond between carbon atoms will produce :
(*a*) Two carbonium ions
(*b*) Two molecules
(*c*) Free radicals
(*d*) Carbonium ion and carbanion
Answer. (*c*)
36. The order of stability of carbonium ions is
(*a*) tertiary > secondary > primary
(*b*) secondary > tertiary > primary
(*c*) primary > secondary > tertiary
(*d*) primary > tertiary > secondary
Answer. (*a*)

37. The order of stability of carbanions is
(*a*) primary > secondary > tertiary
(*b*) secondary > tertiary > primary
(*c*) tertiary > secondary > primary
(*d*) tertiary > primary > secondary
Answer. (*a*)
38. Which of the following carbonium ions will be most stable?
(*a*) $\overset{+}{C}H_3$
(*b*) $CH_3\overset{+}{C}H_2$
(*c*) $(CH_3)_2\overset{+}{C}H$
(*d*) $CH_2{=}CH\overset{+}{C}H_2$
Answer. (*d*)
39. The least stable carbanion is :
(*a*) $C_6H_5\overset{-}{C}H_2$
(*b*) $(CH_3)_3\overset{-}{C}$
(*c*) $\overset{-}{C}Cl_3$
(*d*) $\overset{-}{C}H_3$
Answer. (*b*)
40. Which alkyl free radical is the most stable?
(*a*) methyl
(*b*) primary
(*c*) secondary
(*d*) tertiary
Answer. (*d*)
41. Which of the following is an electrophile?
(*a*) $CH_3\overset{-}{O}$
(*b*) $CH_3\overset{+}{C}H_2$
(*c*) NH_3
(*d*) $CH_3\overset{-}{C}H_2$
Answer. (*b*)
42. Which of the following is not an electrophile?
(*a*) NH_3

(*b*) Br^+
(*c*) $AlCl_3$
(*d*) NO_2^+
Answer. (*a*)
43. Which of the following statements is correct regarding nucleophiles?
(*a*) They have an overall positive charge
(*b*) They have a lone-pair of electrons
(*c*) They have an unpaired electron
(*d*) They have empty orbitals
Answer. (*b*)
44. Which of the following is a nucleophile?
(*a*) $AlCl_3$
(*b*) H_3O+
(*c*) BF_3
(*d*) CN^-
Answer. (*d*)
45. Which of the following is not a nucleophile?
(*a*) NH_3
(*b*) HSO_3^-
(*c*) $AlCl_3$
(*d*) HO^-
Answer. (*c*)
46. Which of the following is not a nucleophile?
(*a*) $\bar{C}N$
(*b*) BF_3
(*c*) $CH_3\bar{O}$
(*d*) NH_3
Answer. (*b*)
47. Which of the following is a Lewis acid?
(*a*) $AlCl_3$
(*b*) CH_3OH
(*c*) NH_3
(*d*) CH_3OCH_3
Answer. (*a*)

48. Which of the following ranges best represents the strength of a hydrogen bond?
(*a*) 5-10 kcals
(*b*) 60-80 kcals
(*c*) 80-100 kcals
(*d*) 100-120 kcals
Answer. (*a*)
49. Which describes the bond strength or bond dissociation energy?
(*a*) energy required to break a bond
(*b*) energy released when a bond breaks
(*c*) energy released when a bond is formed
(*d*) (*a*) and (*c*)
Answer. (*d*)
50. Which statement is correct?
(*a*) Energy is released when a bond breaks.
(*b*) A sigma bond results from attraction of protons and electrons.
(*c*) Energy is released when a bond forms.
(*d*) A carbanion is positively charged.
Answer. (*c*)
51. Which of the following is *incorrect?*
(*a*) Resonance stabilization is the extra stability a compound gains from having delocalized electrons.
(*b*) Delocalized electrons destabilize a compound.
(*c*) The greater the number of relatively stable resonance contributors, the greater is the resonance stabilization.
(*d*) (*a*) and (*c*)
Answer. (*b*)
52. Which of the following is correct?
(*a*) Curved arrows are always drawn from an electron poor center to an electron rich center.
(*b*) A doubled headed arrow means one electron has been moved.
(*c*) Curved arrows are always drawn from an electron rich center to an electron poor center.

(*d*) A single headed arrow means two electrons have been moved.

Answer. (*c*)

53. What does a "curved" arrow represent?

(*a*) that two structures are resonance structures
(*b*) the movement of two electrons
(*c*) a link between reactants and products
(*d*) that two structures are equivalent

Answer. (*b*)

54. What is the predicted shape, bond angle, and hybridization for CH_3^+?

(*a*) trigonal planar, 120°, sp^2
(*b*) trigonal planar, 120°, sp^3
(*c*) trigonal planar, 109.5°, sp^2
(*d*) trigonal pyramidal, 120°, sp^2

Answer. (*a*)

55. What is the name given for a species that contains a positively charged carbon atom?

(*a*) carbanion
(*b*) carbocation
(*c*) methyl radical
(*d*) free radical

Answer. (*c*)

56. What orbitals overlap to create the H–C bond in CH_3^+?

(*a*) sp^3–sp^3
(*b*) sp^2–sp^3
(*c*) *s*–*p*
(*d*) *s*–sp^2

Answer. (*d*)

57. The lone-pair electrons of the methyl anion occupy a __________ orbital.

(a) *s*
(*b*) *sp*
(*c*) sp^2
(*d*) sp^3

Answer. (*d*)

58. An increase in which of the following results in a decrease in the rate of the chemical reaction?
(*a*) temperature
(*b*) concentration
(*c*) collision frequency
(*d*) energy of activation
Answer. (*d*)
59. The reaction step that has its transition state at the highest point on the reaction coordinate is the called the __________.
(*a*) rate-determining step
(*b*) activation energy
(*c*) transition step
(*d*) product favored step
Answer. (*a*)
60. An electrophile acts as a __________ when it reacts with a nucleophile.
(*a*) Bronsted-Lowry base
(*b*) Arrhenius base
(*c*) Lewis acid
(*d*) Lewis base
Answer. (*c*)
61. A nucleophile acts as a __________ when it reacts with an electrophile.
(*a*) Bronsted-Lowry acid
(*b*) Arrhenius base
(*c*) Lewis acid
(*d*) Lewis base
Answer. (*d*)
62. Which of the following is *not* normally considered to be a nucleophile?
(*a*) NH_3
(*b*) CH_3NH_2
(*c*) $HC{\equiv}C:^-$
(*d*) $CH_3CH_2^+$
Answer. (*d*)

63. Which of the following is *not* a nucleophile?
(*a*) $FeBr_3$
(*b*) Br^-
(*c*) NH_3
(*d*) CH_3OCH_3
Answer. (*a*)
64. Which of the following is the strongest interaction?
(*a*) a covalent bond
(*b*) dipole-dipole interactions
(*c*) hydrogen bonding
(*d*) van der Waals
Answer. (*a*)
65. Which of the following statements is *incorrect*?
(*a*) Electrons move toward positively charged locations.
(*b*) An electron-rich atom is called an electrophile.
(*c*) An electrophile is electron loving.
(*d*) A nucleophile has a a pair of electrons it can share.
Answer. (*b*)
66. Which of the following is a nonpolar molecule?
(*a*) HCl
(*b*) CH_3Cl
(*c*) H_2
(*d*) NH_3
Answer. (*c*)
67. Which is defined as a species that accepts a proton?
(*a*) Lewis acid
(*b*) Lewis base
(*c*) Bronsted-Lowry acid
(*d*) Bronsted-Lowry base
Answer. (*d*)
68. Which statement is correct about acid-base chemistry?
(*a*) the larger the K_a, the stronger the acid
(*b*) a small pK_a correspond to a large K_a
(*c*) the smaller the pK_a, the stronger the acid
(*d*) all of the above
Answer. (*d*)

69. Which of the following statements is correct?
(*a*) The stronger the acid, the weaker its conjugate base.
(*b*) The stronger the acid, the stronger its conjugate base.
(*c*) The stronger the base, the stronger its conjugate base.
(*d*) The stronger the acid, the weaker its conjugate acid.
Answer. (*a*)
70. What is the conjugate acid of CH_3NH_2?
(*a*) $CH_3NH_3^+$
(*b*) CH_3NH^-
(*c*) NH_4^+
(*d*) NH_2^-
Answer. (*a*)
71. What is the conjugate base of CH_3NH_2?
(*a*) $CH_3NH_3^+$
(*b*) CH_3NH^-
(*c*) NH_4^+
(*d*) NH_2^-
Answer. (*b*)
72. The stronger the acid __________.
(*a*) the less stable its conjugate base
(*b*) the larger the pK_a
(*c*) the weaker its conjugate base
(*d*) the larger the *p*H
Answer. (*c*)
73. Which of the following is the strongest acid?
(*a*) HI
(*b*) H_2O
(*c*) CH_4
(*d*) CH_3OH
Answer. (*a*)
74. Which of the following are Lewis bases?
(*a*) NF_3
(*b*) BF_3
(*c*) CH_3OCH_3
(*d*) (*a*) and (*c*)
Answer. (*d*)

75. Two compounds have the same composition and also have the same atoms attached to the same atoms, although with different orientations in space. These compounds are
(*a*) Identical
(*b*) Position isomers
(*c*) Structural isomers
(*d*) Stereoisomers
Answer. (*d*)
76. The isomers of a substance must have
(*a*) same chemical properties
(*b*) same molecular weight
(*c*) same structural formula
(*d*) same functional groups
Answer. (*b*)
77. Compounds with the same molecular formula but different structural formulas are called
(*a*) Alkoxides
(*b*) Iso compounds
(*c*) Isomers
(*d*) Ortho compounds
Answer. (*c*)
78. Ethanol (CH_3CH_2OH) and dimethyl ether (CH_3OCH_3) are best considered :
(*a*) structural isomers
(*b*) stereoisomers
(*c*) enantiomers
(*d*) diastereomers
Answer. (*a*)
79. The compounds $CH_3CH_2OCH_2CH_3$ and $CH_3OCH_2CH_2CH_3$ are
(*a*) Enantiomers
(*b*) Conformational isomers
(*c*) Metamers
(*d*) Optical isomers
Answer. (*c*)

80. Which of the following statements is false about tautomers?
(*a*) Tautomers are structural isomers
(*b*) Tautomers are structural isomers which exist in dynamic equilibrium
(*c*) Tautomerism involves movement of atoms
(*d*) Tautomers have independent existence
Answer. (*d*)
81. How many isomers are possible for the compound with molecular formula C_4H_8?
(*a*) 2
(*b*) 4
(*c*) 6
(*d*) 8
Answer. (*c*)
82. How many structural isomers are possible for C_4H_9Br?
(*a*) 2
(*b*) 3
(*c*) 4
(*d*) 5
Answer. (c)
83. How many isomeric aromatic hydrocarbons are possible for C_8H_{10}?
(*a*) 3
(*b*) 4
(*c*) 5
(*d*) 6
Answer. (*b*)
84. Which compound is not an isomer of the other three?
(*a*) *n*-Pentane
(*b*) 2,2-Dimethylpropane
(*c*) 2-Methylbutane
(*d*) 2,3-Dimethylbutane
Answer. (*d*)
85. Alkenes show geometrical isomerism due to :
(*a*) Asymmetry

(*b*) Rotation around a single bond
(*c*) Resonance
(*d*) Restricted rotation around a double bond
Answer. (*d*)
86. Which of the following compounds exhibit geometrical isomerism?
(*a*) 1-Pentene
(*b*) 2-Methyl-2-pentene
(*c*) 2-Pentene
(*d*) 2-Methyl-2-butene
Answer. (*c*)
87. Which of the following compounds may exist as *cis-trans* isomers?
(*a*) 1-Butene
(*b*) 2-Butene
(*c*) Cyclopropane
(*d*) Acetone
Answer. (*b*)
88. Geometrical isomerism is shown by
(*a*) Lactic acid
(*b*) Maleic acid
(*c*) 1-Butene
(*d*) 1,1-Dichloroethylene
Answer. (*b*)
89. Which of the following compounds show geometrical isomerism
(*a*) $(CH_3)_3N$
(*b*) $CH_3CH{=}CH_2$
(*c*) $(CH_3)_2NH$
(*d*) $CH_3CH{=}CHCH_3$
Answer. (*d*)
90. Which of the following compounds will show geometrical isomerism?
(*a*) $CH_2{=}CHCl_2$
(*b*) $ClCH{=}CHBr$
(*c*) $CH_2{=}CHCl$

(*d*) $Cl_2C=CBr_2$
Answer. (*b*)
91. Which of the following compounds will not show geometrical isomerism?
(*a*) $BrCH=CHBr$
(*b*) $BrCH=CHCl$
(*c*) $CH_3-C(Br)=CHBr$
(*d*) $CH_3-C(CH_3)=CHCH_3$
Answer. (*d*)
92. A molecule is said to be chiral
(*a*) if it contains plane of symmetry
(*b*) if it contains centre of symmetry
(*c*) if it cannot be superimposed on its mirror image
(*d*) if it can be superimposed on its mirror image
Answer. (*c*)
93. Which of the statements is false regarding chiral compounds?
(*a*) rotate the plane of polarized light
(*b*) have cis and trans isomers
(*c*) exist as enantiomers
(*d*) can be detected with a polarimeter
Answer. (*b*)
94. An optically active compound
(*a*) must contain atleast four carbons
(*b*) when in solution rotate the plane of polarized light
(*c*) must always contain an asymmetric carbon atom
(*d*) in solution always give a negative reading in polarimeter.
Answer. (*b*)
95. Plane-polarized light is affected by
(*a*) Identical molecules
(*b*) All polymers
(*c*) Chiral molecules
(*d*) All biomolecules

Answer. (*c*)
96. It is possible to distinguish between optical isomers
(*a*) by using chemical tests
(*b*) by mass spectrometry
(*c*) by IR spectroscopy
(*d*) by polarimetry
Answer. (*d*)
97. Optical isomers that are mirror images are called :
(*a*) Tautomers
(*b*) Diastereomers
(*c*) Enantiomers
(*d*) Metamers
Answer. (*c*)
98. Optical isomers that are not mirror images are called
(*a*) Diastereomers
(*b*) Enantiomers
(*c*) Metamers
(*d*) Meso compounds
Answer. (*a*)
99. Enantiomers have which of the following characteristics?
(*a*) rotate ordinary light
(*b*) have the same melting point
(*c*) are superimposable mirror images
(*d*) react with optically active molecules at the same rate
Answer. (*b*)
100. Which of the following statements is false about enantiomers?
(*a*) rotate plane-polarized light
(*b*) are superimposable mirror images
(*c*) are nonsuperimposable mirror images
(*d*) have the same melting point
Answer. (*b*)
101. A meso compound :
(*a*) is an achiral molecule which contains chiral carbons
(*b*) contains a plane of symmetry or a centre of symmetry

(*c*) is optically inactive
(*d*) is characterized by all of the above
Answer. (*d*)
102. What is the possible number of optical isomers for a compound containing *n* dissimilar asymmetric carbon atoms?
(*a*) n^2
(*b*) 2^n
(*c*) $n + 1$
(*d*) $n + 2$
Answer. (*b*)
103. What is the possible number of optical isomers for a compound containing 2 dissimilar asymmetric carbon atoms?
(*a*) 2
(*b*) 4
(*c*) 6
(*d*) 8
Answer. (*b*)
104. *meso*-Tartaric acid is
(*a*) sometimes optically active
(*b*) always optically active
(*c*) sometimes optically inactive
(*d*) always optically inactive
Answer. (*d*)
105. Which of the following compounds will be optically active?
(*a*) Propanoic acid
(*b*) 3-Chloropropanoic acid
(*c*) 2-Chloropropanoic acid
(*d*) 3-Chloropropene
Answer. (*c*)
106. Which of the following compounds will be optically active?
(*a*) Succinic acid
(*b*) *meso*-Tartaric acid

(*d*) Lactic acid
(*d*) Chloroacetic acid
Answer. (*c*)
107. Which of the following isomeric compounds show optical isomerism :
(*a*) 1-Aminopentane
(*b*) 2-Aminopentane
(*c*) 3-Aminopentane
(*d*) 2,2-Dimethylpropylamine
Answer. (*b*)
108. 2-Butanol is optically active because it contains :
(*a*) an asymmetric carbon
(*b*) a plane of symmetry
(*c*) a hydroxyl group
(*d*) a centre of symmetry
Answer. (*a*)
109. Optical isomerism is shown by
(*a*) *n*-Butyl chloride
(*b*) *sec*-Butyl chloride
(*c*) *tert*-Butyl chloride
(*d*) Isobutyl chloride
Answer. (*b*)
110. Which of the following compounds is an optically active compound?
(*a*) $CH_3-\underset{}{\overset{OH}{\overset{|}{C}}}H-COOH$
(*b*) $CHCl_3$
(*c*) CH_3CH_2COOH
(*d*) CH_3CH_2OH
Answer. (*a*)
111. Lactic acid, $CH_3-\overset{OH}{\overset{|}{C}}H-COOH$, is a molecule which shows
(*a*) Geometrical isomerism
(*b*) Tautomerism
(*c*) Optical isomerism

(*d*) Metamerism
Answer. (*c*)
112. How many optical isomers are possible for lactic acid?
(*a*) 2
(*b*) 4
(*c*) 6
(*d*) 8
Answer. (*a*)
113. Which of the following represents a racemic mixture?
(*a*) 75% (R)-2-butanol, 25% (S)-2-butanol
(*b*) 25% (R)-2-butanol, 75% (S)-2-butanol
(*c*) 50% (R)-2-butanol, 50% (S)-2-butanol
(*d*) none of the above
Answer. (*c*)
114. Consider (R)- and (S)-2-butanol. Which physical property distinguishes the two compounds?
(*a*) melting point
(*b*) solubility in common solvents
(*c*) Rotation of plane-polarized light
(*d*) Infrared spectrum
Answer. (*c*)
115. Which of the following is capable of exhibiting *cis-trans* isomerism?
(*a*) 1-butene
(*b*) 1-pentene
(*c*) ethene
(*d*) 2-butene
Answer. (*d*)
116. Which of the following is a true statement?
(*a*) All chiral molecules possess a plane of symmetry.
(*b*) All achiral molecules are meso.
(*c*) All molecules which possess a single asymmetric center of the S configuration are levorotatory.
(*d*) A mixture of achiral compounds will be optically inactive.
Answer. (*d*)

117. Which of the statements below correctly describes an achiral molecule?
(*a*) The molecule has a nonsuperimposable mirror image.
(*b*) The molecule exhibits optical activity when it interacts with plane-polarized light.
(*c*) The molecule has an enantiomer.
(*d*) The molecule might be a meso form.
Answer. (*d*)
118. How many asymmetric centers are present in a molecule of 2,4,6-trimethylheptane?
(*a*) 0
(*b*) 1
(*c*) 2
(*d*) 3
Answer. (*a*)
119. Which of the following compounds is never chiral?
(*a*) 2,3-dibromobutane
(*b*) 1,3-dibromobutane
(*c*) 1,2-dichlorobutane
(*d*) 1,4-dibromobutane
Answer. (*d*)
120. Which of the following statements is correct concerning a pair of enantiomers?
(*a*) They rotate the plane of polarized light by exactly the same amount and in opposite directions.
(*b*) They rotate the plane of polarized light by differing amounts and in opposite directions.
(*c*) They rotate the plane of polarized light by differing amounts and in the same direction.
(*d*) They have different melting points.
Answer. (*a*)
121. Which of the following is *not* true of enantiomers?
(*a*) They have the same melting point.
(*b*) They have the same boiling point.
(*c*) They have the same density.
(*d*) They have the same specific rotation.

Answer. (*d*)

122. A and B are stereoisomers. They are nonsuperimposable and are mirror images of one another. Which of the following best describes the relationship between A and B?

(*a*) structural isomers
(*b*) enantiomers
(*c*) *cis-trans* isomers
(*d*) diastereomers

Answer. (*b*)

123. Which of the statements is correct about diastereomers?

(*a*) They are stereoisomers that are not enantiomers.
(*b*) They are a pair of identical isomers.
(*c*) They are a pair of isomers that are mirror images.
(*d*) All their asymmetric centers are the same.

Answer. (*a*)

124. Which of the following is/are optically inactive?

(*a*) a 50-50 mixture of R and S enantiomers
(*b*) a meso compound
(*c*) a racemic mixture
(*d*) all the above

Answer. (*d*)

125. Hydrocarbons are

(*a*) Composed of carbon and hydrogen
(*b*) Composed of carbon, hydrogen, and oxygen
(*c*) Composed of carbon and oxygen
(*d*) Composed of carbon and nitrogen

Answer. (*a*)

126. Hydrocarbons are

(*a*) insoluble in water
(*b*) composed of carbon and hydrogen
(*c*) both (*a*) and (*b*)
(*d*) None of these

Answer. (*c*)

127. Which of following statements is false about propane?

(*a*) all bond angles are 109.5°
(*b*) each carbon is *sp*3 hybridized
(*c*) the compound is combustible
(*d*) the compound undergoes polymerization to give polypropylene.
Answer. (*d*)
128. Which of the following is a correct name according to the IUPAC rules?
(*a*) 2-Methylcyclohexane
(*b*) 2-Ethyl-2-methylpentane
(*c*) 3,4-Dimethylpentane
(*d*) 3-Ethyl-2-methylpentane
Answer. (*d*)
129. A tertiary carbon is bonded directly to :
(*a*) 2 hydrogens
(*b*) 3 carbons
(*c*) 2 carbons
(*d*) 4 carbons
Answer. (*b*)
130. What type of an alkyl group is an isobutyl group?
(*a*) primary
(*b*) secondary
(*c*) tertiary
(*d*) none of these
Answer. (*a*)
131. Which molecular formula indicates 2-methylpentane?
(*a*) C_5H_{12}
(*b*) C_6H_{14}
(*c*) C_5H_{10}
(*d*) C_6H_{12}
Answer. (*b*)
132. Which molecular formula indicates 2,2,4-trimethylhexane?
(*a*) C_9H_{20}
(*b*) C_9H_{18}
(*c*) C_8H_{18}

(*d*) C_8H_{16}
Answer. (*a*)
133. How many isomers are possible for butane?
(*a*) 2
(*b*) 3
(*c*) 4
(*d*) 5
Answer. (*a*)
134. How many isomers are possible for 2-methylpropane?
(*a*) 2
(*b*) 3
(*c*) 4
(*d*) 5
Answer. (*a*)
135. How many isomers are possible for pentane?
(*a*) 2
(*b*) 3
(*c*) 4
(*d*) 5
Answer. (*b*)
136. How many isomers are possible for hexane?
(*a*) 4
(*b*) 5
(*c*) 6
(*d*) 7
Answer. (*b*)
137. How many isomers are possible for heptane?
(*a*) 9
(*b*) 10
(*c*) 11
(*d*) 12
Answer. (*a*)
138. Marsh gas mainly contains
(*a*) $CH_2=CH_2$
(*b*) CH_4
(*c*) H_2S

(*d*) $CHCl_3$
Answer. (*b*)
139. Which statement is false?
(*a*) Many alkanes are soluble in water.
(*b*) All alkanes have a lower density than water.
(*c*) At room temperature some alkanes are liquids, some solids, some gases.
(*d*) All alkanes burn.
Answer. (*a*)
140. As the molecular weight of alkanes increases, how do the boiling point and melting point change?
(*a*) boiling point increases ; melting point increases.
(*b*) boiling point increases ; melting point increases.
(*c*) boiling point increases ; melting point decreases
(*d*) boiling point increases ; melting point increases sequentially for alkanes over four carbons.
Answer. (*d*)
141. The branching of alkanes that produces symmetrical structures :
(*a*) raises the boiling point ; raises the melting point
(*b*) raises the boiling point ; lowers the melting point
(*c*) lowers the boiling point ; lowers the melting point
(*d*) lowers the boiling point ; raises the melting point
Answer. (*a*)
142. How does the melting point of propane and ethane compare?
(*a*) the melting point of propane is greater.
(*b*) the melting point of ethane is greater.
(*c*) the melting points are within 5°C of one another.
(*d*) no relationship exists among these alkanes and their melting points.
Answer. (*b*)
143. How do the boiling points of butane, propane, and ethane compare?
(*a*) the boiling point of ethane is greatest.
(*b*) the boiling point of butane is greatest.

(*c*) the boiling point of propane is greatest.
(*d*) there is no relationship among these three alkanes and their boiling points.
Answer. (*b*)
144. Which of the following alkanes will have the *highest* boiling point?
(*a*) *n*-Octane
(*b*) Isopentane
(*c*) *n*-Butane
(*d*) Neopentane
Answer. (*a*)
145. Which of the following alkanes will have the *lowest* boiling point?
(*a*) *n*-Heptane
(*b*) Isopentane
(*c*) *n*-Hexane
(*d*) Neopentane
Answer. (*d*)
146. Methane can be prepared by :
(*a*) the reaction of iodomethane with sodium in dry ether
(*b*) the reaction of methanol with concentrated H_2SO_4
(*c*) the reaction of sodium methanoate with soda-lime
(*d*) the reaction of sodium ethanoate with soda-lime
Answer. (*d*)
147. Which of the following reactions can be used to prepare alkanes?
(*a*) Corey-House synthesis
(*b*) Williamson synthesis
(*c*) Friedel-Crafts reactions
(*d*) None of these
Answer. (*a*)
148. Which of the following reactions can be used to prepare alkanes?
(*a*) Wurtz reaction
(*b*) Wolf-kishner reduction
(*c*) Kolbe's electrolysis

(*d*) All of these
Answer. (*d*)
149. Kolbe's electrolysis of sodium butyrate gives
(*a*) C_8H_{16}
(*b*) C_6H_{14}
(*c*) C_8H_{18}
(*d*) C_6H_{12}
Answer. (*b*)
150. Which of the following classes of compounds is unreactive toward sulfuric acid?
(*a*) Alkanes
(*b*) Alcohols
(*c*) Alkenes
(*d*) Alkynes
Answer. (*a*)
151. Which of the following compounds does not dissolve in concentrated H_2SO_4 on warming?
(*a*) *n*-Hexane
(*b*) Diethyl ether
(*c*) 1-Butene
(*d*) Aniline
Answer. (*a*)
152. 2,3-Dimethyl-2-butene undergoes catalytic hydrogenation to give
(*a*) 2,3-Dimethylbutane
(*b*) 2-Methylpentane
(*c*) 2,2-Dimethylbutane
(*d*) 3-Methylpentane
Answer. (*a*)
153. Why is the halogenation of alkanes considered a chain reaction?
(*a*) it occurs quickly.
(*b*) it occurs without the generation of intermediates.
(*c*) each step generates the reactive intermediate that causes the next step to occur.

(*d*) the reaction allows long chains of halogenated alkanes to be formed.
Answer. (*c*)
154. The chlorination of methane to give CCl_4 is an example of
(*a*) an electrophilic addition
(*b*) a free-radical substitution
(*c*) a nucleophilic addition
(*d*) an electrophilic substitution
Answer. (*b*)
155. In the chlorination of alkanes, the first step in which chlorine free radicals are produced is called :
(*a*) initiation
(*b*) activation
(*c*) propagation
(*d*) deactivation
Answer. (*a*)
156. Chlorine free radicals react with methane by :
(*a*) donating their free-radical electron to methane to form chloromethane.
(*b*) abstracting a hydrogen atom from methane, and producing HCl and a methyl radical.
(*c*) forming a carbanion intermediate that rapidly dissociates to produce chloromethane.
(*d*) forming a carbonium ion intermediate that rapidly dissociates to form chloromethane.
Answer. (*b*)
157. Which halogen *does not* appreciably react with methane in a free-radical substitution reaction?
(*a*) chlorine
(*b*) bromine
(*c*) iodine
(*d*) fluorine
Answer. (*c*)
158. What product is formed in the free-radical bromination of methane?

(*a*) bromomethane
(*b*) dibromomethane
(c) tribromomethane
(*d*) all of these
Answer. (*d*)
159. Chlorination of an alkane as compared to bromination proceeds
(*a*) at a slower rate
(*b*) at a faster rate
(*c*) with equal rates
(*d*) with equal or different rate depending upon the source of alkane.
Answer. (*b*)
160. How many monochlorinated isomers would result from the reaction of chlorine with *n*-butane in the presence of UV light?
(*a*) 2
(*b*) 4
(*c*) 6
(*d*) 8
Answer. (*a*)
161. How many monochlorination products are possible in the reaction of 2,2-dimethylbutane with chlorine in the presence of ultraviolet light?
(*a*) 2
(*b*) 3
(*c*) 4
(*d*) 5
Answer. (*a*)
162. A compound of formula C_3H_8 does not react with bromine in CCl_4 in the dark. The compound could be
(*a*) Alkane
(*b*) Cycloalkane
(*c*) Alkene
(*d*) Cycloalkene
Answer. (*a*)

163. The combustion of Pentane produces :
(*a*) Pentene
(*b*) HCl + H_2O
(*c*) Pentyne
(*d*) CO_2 + H_2O
Answer. (*d*)
164. The combustion of one mole of propane, C_3H_8, produces how many moles of H_2O?
(*a*) 2
(*b*) 3
(*c*) 4
(*d*) 5
Answer. (*c*)
165. The major carbon compound formed from the incomplete combustion of a hydrocarbon in air is
(*a*) carbon dioxide
(*b*) carbon monoxide
(*c*) water
(*d*) alkyl chains
Answer. (*b*)
166. The thermal decomposition of alkanes in the absence of air is called :
(*a*) Combustion
(*b*) Oxidation
(*c*) Cracking
(*d*) Hydrogenation
Answer. (*c*)
167. LPG (Household cooking gas) is mainly a mixture of
(*a*) Methane + Ethane
(*b*) Acetylene + O_2
(*c*) Butane + Isobutane
(*d*) Acetylene + H_2
Answer. (*c*)
168. What type of bonding is most important in $CH_3CH_2CH_2CH_2CH_2CH_3$?
(*a*) ionic

(*b*) hydrogen
(*c*) covalent
(*d*) polar
Answer. (*c*)
169. What is the name given to a compound containing only carbons and hydrogens and having the maximum number of hydrogens in the molecule?
(*a*) alkene
(*b*) unsaturated hydrocarbon
(*c*) saturated hydrocarbon
(*d*) alkyne
Answer. (*c*)
170. Which of the following is the best description of propane, $CH_3CH_2CH_3$, at room temperature?
(*a*) liquid, soluble in H_2O
(*b*) gas, soluble in gasoline
(*c*) liquid, soluble in gasoline
(*d*) gas, soluble in water
Answer. (*b*)
171. Choose the correct hybridization for the atom indicated in the molecule below.

$$\underset{\uparrow}{C}H_3CH_2CH_2CH_3$$

(*a*) *sp*
(*b*) sp^2
(*c*) sp^3
(*d*) none of these
Answer. (*c*)
172. Which of the following has the greatest solubility in $CH_3CH_2CH_2CH_3$?
(*a*) CH_3OH
(*b*) CH_3NH_2
(*c*) CH_3OCH_3
(*d*) $(CH_3)_3CH$
Answer. (*d*)

173. Consider the three isomeric alkanes *n*-hexane, 2,3-dimethylbutane, and 2-methylpentane. Which of the following correctly lists these compounds in order of increasing boiling point?
(*a*) 2,3-dimethylbutane < 2-methylpentane < *n*-hexane
(*b*) 2-methylpentane < *n*-hexane < 2,3-dimethylbutane
(*c*) 2-methylpentane < 2, 3-dimethylbutane < *n*-hexane
(*d*) *n*-hexane < 2-methylpentane < 2,3-dimethylbutane
Answer. (*a*)
174. The eclipsed and staggered forms of ethane are said to differ in _________.
(*a*) molecular formula
(*b*) configuration
(*c*) conformation
(*d*) constitution
Answer. (*c*)
175. Octane number is related to
(*a*) Gasoline
(*b*) Kerosene oil
(*c*) Diesel oil
(*d*) Lubricating oil
Answer. (*a*)
176. A knocking sound is produced in the engine when the fuel
(*a*) Burns fast
(*b*) contains lubricating oil
(*c*) Burns slow
(*d*) contains water
Answer. (*a*)
177. The octane rating of gasoline provides information on
(*a*) its antiknock properties
(*b*) its ignition properties
(*c*) its percentage proportion of octane
(*d*) its percentage content of isooctane
Answer. (*a*)

178. In any fuel, the percentage by volume of isooctane in a mixture of isooctane and *n*-heptane which will knock under same conditions as the fuel being tested, is called :
(*a*) Cracking
(*b*) Iodine number
(*c*) Aromatization
(*d*) Octane number
Answer. (*d*)
179. Which of the following compounds is assigned the Octane Number of zero :
(*a*) *n*-Octane
(*b*) 2,3,3-Trimethylpentane
(*c*) *n*-Heptane
(*d*) 2,2,4-Trimethylpentane
Answer. (*c*)
180. Which of the following compounds is assigned the Octane Number of 100 :
(*a*) *n*-Heptane
(*b*) 2,3,3-Trimethylpentane
(*c*) *n*-Octane
(*d*) 2,2,4-Trimethylpentane
Answer. (*d*)
181. Gasoline with an octane number of 90 is equivalent in knocking characteristics to a mixture of heptane and isooctane of the following composition :
(*a*) 20% heptane + 80% isooctane
(*b*) 90% heptane + 10% isooctane
(*c*) 80% heptane + 20% isooctane
(*d*) 10% heptane + 90% isooctane
Answer. (*d*)
182. A fuel with octane number 90 means it is as good as a mixture of :
(*a*) 90% Isooctane + 10% *n*-heptane
(*b*) 90% *n*-Heptane + 10% isooctane
(*c*) 2 Litre of 90% isooctane + 2 litre of benzene
(*d*) 2 Litre of 90% *n*-heptane + 2 litre of benzene

Answer. (*a*)
183. Which hydrocarbon molecule with eight carbons would produce the lowest octane number (i.e., the most knocking) when used as a fuel in automobile?
(*a*) 2-Methyl-3,3-dimethylpentane
(*b*) *n*-Octane
(*c*) 2-Isopropylpentane
(*d*) 2-Methylheptane
Answer. (*b*)
184. Which of the following compounds is used as an antiknock compound?
(*a*) Ethyllithium
(*b*) Tetraethyllead
(*c*) Ethyl acetate
(*d*) Lead acetate
Answer. (*b*)
185. Which of the following methods can be used to increase the octane rating of gasoline?
(*a*) Adding branched-chain alkanes
(*b*) Adding tetraethyllead
(*c*) Adding aromatic hydrocarbons
(*d*) All of these
Answer. (*d*)
186. The carbon atoms involved in the double bond of an alkene are
(*a*) *sp* hybridized
(*b*) sp^2 hybridized
(*c*) sp^3 hybridized
(*d*) None of these
Answer. (*b*)
187. Which of the following compounds will show geometrical isomerism?
(*a*) Propene
(*b*) 2-Butene
(*c*) Propyne
(*d*) 2-Butyne

Answer. (*b*)
188. Which of the following compounds is most stable?
(*a*) Ethylene
(*b*) 2,3-Dimethyl-1-butene
(*c*) Propylene
(*d*) 2-Butene
Answer. (*b*)
189. In which solvent are alkenes most soluble?
(*a*) water
(*b*) ethyl alcohol
(*c*) ammonia
(*d*) carbon tetrachloride
Answer. (*d*)
190. Which statements about alkenes and alkanes of corresponding chain lengths is true?
(I) Alkenes have slightly lower melting points than alkanes
(II) Alkenes have slightly higher melting points than alkanes
(III) Alkenes have higher boiling points than alkanes
(IV) Alkenes have lower boiling points than alkanes
(*a*) I and III
(*b*) II and IV
(*c*) I and IV
(*d*) II and III
Answer. (*a*)
191. How do the melting points of *trans* isomers compare to the *cis* isomers for alkenes?
(*a*) *cis* isomers have higher melting points
(*b*) *trans* isomers have higher melting points
(*c*) both have similar melting points
(*d*) no consistent trend is observed
Answer. (*b*)
192. Why do *trans* isomers of alkenes have lower boiling points than *cis* isomers?
(*a*) *trans* isomers have better symmetry
(*b*) *cis* isomers have better symmetry
(*c*) *trans* isomers are less polar

(*d*) *cis* isomers are less polar
Answer. (*c*)
193. The major product of acid-catalyzed dehydration of 3-pentanol is :
(*a*) 1-Pentene
(*b*) 2-Methyl-1-butene
(*c*) 2-Pentene
(*d*) 3-Methyl-1-butene
Answer. (*c*)
194. Ethylene is obtained from ethyl bromide by :
(*a*) Simple heating
(*b*) Hydrolysis
(*c*) Dehydrohalogenation
(*d*) Nucleophilic substitution
Answer. (*c*)
195. The dehydrohalogenation of 2-bromobutane with alcoholic KOH gives mainly
(*a*) 2-Butene
(*b*) 2-Butyne
(*c*) 1-Butene
(*d*) 1-Butyne
Answer. (*a*)
196. In the reaction of propene with HCl, H+ ion acts as the :
(*a*) electrophile
(*b*) carbonium ion
(*c*) nucleophile
(*d*) carbanion
Answer. (*a*)
197. When bromine attacks the double bond in propene, which of the following ions is formed in the first stage of the attack?
(*a*) $CH_3-\overset{+}{C}H-CH_2Br$
(*b*) $CH_3-\underset{}{\overset{\overset{\large Br}{|}}{C}H}-\overset{+}{C}H_2$

(*c*) $CH_3-\ddot{C}H-CH_2Br$

(*d*) $CH_3-CH(Br)-\ddot{C}H_2$

Answer. (*a*)

198. In the reaction of ethylene with H2O in the presence of sulfuric acid, which one adds across the double bond first?

(*a*) H^+

(*b*) H·

(*c*) HO^-

(*d*) sulfate ion

Answer. (*a*)

199. Why does a H+ ion attacking a carbon-carbon double bond add to the carbon with the least number of substituents?

(*a*) the reaction is resonance stabilized.

(*b*) the hybrid geometry favors this process.

(*c*) nucleophile tends to attack stable centers of negative charge.

(*d*) a more stable carbonium ion is generated.

Answer. (*d*)

200. Propene reacts with bromine to form 1,2-dibromopropane. This is an example of

(*a*) Nucleophilic addition

(*b*) Electrophilic addition

(*c*) Nucleophilic substitution

(*d*) Electrophilic substitution

Answer. (*b*)

201. Baeyer's reagent is

(*a*) dilute $KMnO_4$

(*b*) HCl + $ZnCl_2$

(*c*) Br2 in CCl_4

(*d*) NH_2NH_2

Answer. (*a*)

202. In the addition of HX to a double bond, the hydrogen goes to the carbon that already has more hydrogens is a

statement of
(*a*) Hund's rule
(*b*) Markovnikov's rule
(*c*) Huckel rule
(*d*) Saytzeff rule
Answer. (*b*)
203. Markovnikov's addition of HBr is not applicable to
(*a*) Propene
(*b*) 1-butene
(*c*) 1-pentene
(*d*) 2-butene
Answer. (*d*)
204. In the reaction of $CH_3CH_2CH=CH_2$ with HCl, the H of the HCl will become attached to which carbon?
(*a*) C-1
(*b*) C-2
(*c*) C-3
(*d*) C-4
Answer. (*a*)
205. Which of the following compounds will react most readily with bromine in CCl_4?
(*a*) $CH_3CH_2CH_3$
(*b*) $(CH_3)_3CH$
(*c*) $CH_3CH=CH_2$
(*d*) $(CH_3)_4C$
Answer. (*c*)
206. The disappearance of the purple color of $KMnO_4$ in its reaction with alkene is known as
(*a*) Markovnikov test
(*b*) Grignard test
(*c*) Baeyer test
(*d*) Wurtz test
Answer. (*c*)
207. Which of the following will give a negative test when treated with bromine in carbon tetrachloride?
(*a*) Butane

(*b*) 2-Butene
(*c*) 1,3-Butadiene
(*d*) 2-Butyne
Answer. (*a*)

208. Ethylene reacts with HI to give
(*a*) Iodoethane
(*b*) 2,2-Diiodoethane
(*c*) 1,1-Diiodoethane
(*d*) None of these
Answer. (*a*)

209. Which of the following reagents will react with propene?
(*a*) Hot alkaline $KMnO_4$
(*b*) Sodium metal
(*c*) Cold dilute HNO_3
(*d*) $LiAlH_4$
Answer. (*a*)

210. Which of the following compounds will have zero dipole moment?
(*a*) *cis*-1,2-dibromoethylene
(*b*) 1,1-dibromoethylene
(*c*) *trans*-1,2-dibromoethylene
(*d*) all of these
Answer. (*c*)

211. 2-Methylpropene reacts with HBr to give
(*a*) *tert*-Butyl bromide
(*b*) Isobutane
(*c*) *n*-Butyl bromide
(*d*) None of these
Answer. (*a*)

212. 2-Butene reacts with HBr to give
(*a*) 1-Bromobutane
(*b*) 2,3-Dibromobutane
(*c*) 2-Bromobutane
(*d*) 2,2-Dibromobutane
Answer. (*c*)

213. Which of the following alkenes reacts with HBr in the presence of a peroxide to give *anti*-Markovnikov's product?
(*a*) 1-Butene
(*b*) 2,3-Dimethyl-2-butene
(*c*) 2-Butene
(*d*) 3-Hexene
Answer. (*a*)
214. Propene reacts with HBr in the presence of a peroxide to give
(*a*) *n*-Propyl bromide
(*b*) Allyl bromide
(*c*) Isopropyl bromide
(*d*) Vinyl bromide
Answer. (*a*)
215. 2-Methylpropene reacts with HBr in the presence of peroxide to give
(*a*) A primary alkyl bromide
(*b*) A secondary alkyl bromide
(*c*) A tertiary alkyl bromide
(*d*) A vicinal dibromide
Answer. (*a*)
216. 2-Methyl-2-butene reacts with HBr in the presence of peroxide to give
(*a*) A primary alkyl bromide
(*b*) A secondary alkyl bromide
(*c*) A tertiary alkyl bromide
(*d*) A vicinal dibromide
Answer. (*b*)
217. Hydration of 2-methyl-1-propene (with H_2O/H_2SO_4) gives :
(*a*) $CH_3CH_2CH_2OH$
(*b*) $(CH_3)_3COH$
(*c*) $CH_3CH_2CH_2CH_2OH$
(*d*) $(CH_3)_2CHOH$
Answer. (*b*)

218. A compound reacts with steam in the presence of concentrated H_2SO_4 to give isopropyl alcohol. The compound could be
(*a*) Alkane
(*b*) Alkyne
(*c*) Alkene
(*d*) Allene
Answer. (*c*)
219. Propene reacts with Cl_2 in H_2O to give
(*a*) 1-Chloro-2-propanol
(*b*) 2-Chloro-2-propanol
(*c*) 1-Chloro-1-propanol
(*d*) 2-Chloro-1-propanol
Answer. (*a*)
220. 1-Butene reacts with Cl_2 in H_2O to give
(*a*) 1-Chloro-2-butanol
(*b*) 2-Chloro-2-butanol
(*c*) 1-Chloro-1-butanol
(*d*) 2-Chloro-1-butanol
Answer. (*a*)
221. Catalytic hydrogenation of 3-methyl-1-butene gives :
(*a*) Isobutane
(*b*) 2,2-Dimethylbutane
(*c*) 2-Methylbutane
(*d*) 2,3-Dimethylbutane
Answer. (*c*)
222. Which of the following alkenes gives only acetic acid on oxidation with hot concentrated $KMnO_4$.
(*a*) Ethylene
(*b*) 1-Butene
(*c*) Propene
(*d*) 2-Butene
Answer. (*d*)
223. Which of the following compounds will give only acetaldehyde on ozonolysis?
(*a*) 1-Butene

(*b*) Acetylene
(*c*) 2-Butene
(*d*) Ethylene
Answer. (*c*)
224. Which of the following alkenes will give a mixture of acetone and formaldehyde on ozonolysis?
(*a*) 2-butene
(*b*) 2-methyl-2-butene
(*c*) 1-butene
(*d*) 2-methylpropene
Answer. (*d*)
225. Which of the following alkenes will give a mixture of acetone and acetaldehyde an ozonolysis?
(*a*) 1-butene
(*b*) 2-methyl-2-butene
(*c*) 2-butene
(*d*) 2-methylpropene
Answer. (*b*)
226. A hydrocarbon, C_6H_{12}, on ozonolysis gives only one product which does not give silver mirror with Tollens' reagent. The hydrocarbon is
(*a*) 2,3-Dimethyl-2-butene
(*b*) 2-Hexene
(*c*) 2-Methyl-2-pentene
(*d*) 3-Hexene
Answer. (*a*)
227. Combustion of an alkene with sufficient oxygen will produce
(*a*) carbon dioxide and water
(*b*) carbon monoxide and water
(*c*) only carbon dioxide
(*d*) only carbon monoxide
Answer. (*a*)
228. Which of the following are correct statements concerning unsaturated hydrocarbons?
(*a*) All unsaturated hydrocarbons are insoluble in water.

(*b*) All unsaturated hydrocarbons are soluble in nonpolar solvents.
(*c*) All unsaturated hydrocarbons are more dense than water.
(*d*) (*a*) & (*c*)
Answer. (*d*)
229. How many electrons are involved in a carbon-carbon double bond?
(*a*) 1
(*b*) 2
(*c*) 3
(*d*) 4
Answer. (*d*)
230. Which of the following statements about ethene, C_2H_4, is *incorrect*?
(*a*) The H–C–H bond angles are approximately 109.5°.
(*b*) There is a total of five sigma bonds.
(*c*) The carbon atoms are sp^2 hybridized.
(*d*) The H–C–H bond angles are approximately 120°.
Answer. (*a*)
231. Which of the following statements about propene, $CH_3CH{=}CH_2$, is *correct*?
(*a*) All nine atoms lie in the same plane.
(*b*) The compound has a *cis* and *trans* isomer.
(*c*) There is a total of eight sigma bonds.
(*d*) All the carbon atoms are sp_2 hybridized.
Answer. (*c*)
232. Which of the following is capable of exhibiting *cis-trans* isomerism?
(*a*) 1-butene
(*b*) 1-pentene
(*c*) ethene
(*d*) 2-butene
Answer. (*d*)
233. Which of the following is the most stable alkene?
(*a*) *trans*-3-hexene

(*b*) *cis*-3-hexene
(*c*) 1-hexene
(*d*) (Z)-3-hexene
Answer. (*a*)
234. Which of the alkyl chlorides listed below undergoes dehydrohalogenation in the presence of a strong base to give 2-pentene as the only alkene product?
(*a*) 1-chloropentane
(*b*) 2-chloropentane
(*c*) 3-chloropentane
(*d*) 1-chloro-2-methylbutane
Answer. (*c*)
235. What is the major product from the acid-catalyzed hydration of 2-methyl-2-pentene?
(*a*) 2-methylpentane
(*b*) 2-methyl-1-pentanol
(*c*) 2-methyl-2-pentanol
(*d*) 2-methyl-3-pentanol
Answer. (*c*)
236. 1,2-Butadiene has
(*a*) only *sp* hybridized carbon atoms
(*b*) only *sp*2 hybridized carbon atoms
(*c*) only sp^3 hybridized carbon atoms
(*d*) *sp*, sp^2, sp^3 hybridized carbon atoms
Answer. (*d*)
237. How many σ (sigma) bonds are there in CH_2=CH—CH=CH_2?
(*a*) 3
(*b*) 6
(*c*) 9
(*d*) 12
Answer. (*c*)
238. Propadiene, CH_2=C=CH_2, is
(*a*) a planar compound
(*b*) a cumulated diene
(*c*) an isolated diene

(*d*) a conjugated diene
Answer. (*b*)
239. Which of the following compounds have planar molecules?
(*a*) 1,3-Butadiene
(*b*) Dimethyl ether
(*c*) 1-Butene
(*d*) Allene
Answer. (*a*)
240. Which of the following molecular formulas will correspond to an alkene with two double bonds?
(*a*) C_4H_{10}
(*b*) C_5H_{12}
(*c*) C_6H_{10}
(*d*) C_8H_{16}
Answer. (*c*)
241. 1,3-Butadiene reacts with bromine to mainly give
(*a*) 3,4-Dibromo-1-butene
(*b*) 4-Bromo-1-butene
(*c*) 1,4-Dibromo-2-butene
(*d*) 1-Bromo-2-butene
Answer. (*c*)
242. What descriptive term is applied to the type of diene represented by 1,5-octadiene?
(*a*) conjugated diene
(*b*) cumulated diene
(*c*) isolated diene
(*d*) alkynyl diene
Answer. (*c*)
243. What descriptive term is applied to the type of diene represented by 2,4-hexadiene?
(*a*) conjugated diene
(*b*) cumulated diene
(*c*) isolated diene
(*d*) alkynyl diene
Answer. (*a*)

244. Which of the following statements are correct concerning delocalized electrons?
(*a*) Electrons do not belong to a single atom.
(*b*) Electrons are not confined to a bond between two atoms
(*c*) Electrons are shared by three or more atoms.
(*d*) (*a*), (*b*) and (*c*)
Answer. (*d*)
245. What is the hybridization of the central carbon of allene (1,2-propadiene)?
(*a*) *sp*
(*b*) sp^2
(*c*) sp^3
(*d*) *p*
Answer. (*a*)
246. What compound results from the 1,4-addition of one equivalent of HBr to 1,3-butadiene?
(*a*) 1-bromo-1-butene
(*b*) 2-bromo-2-butene
(*c*) 4-bromo-1-butene
(*d*) 1-bromo-2-butene
Answer. (*d*)
247. Rank the following dienes in order of increasing stability :
trans-1, 3-pentadiene, *cis*-1,3-pentadiene, 1,4-pentadiene and 1,2-pentadiene.
Answer. 1,2-pentadiene < 1,4-pentadiene < *cis*-1,3-pentadiene < *trans*-1,3-pentadiene
248. A triple bond consists of
(*a*) 2 *sigma* bonds and 1 *pi* bond
(*b*) 3 *sigma* bonds
(*c*) 1 *sigma* bond and 2 *pi* bonds
(*d*) 3 *pi* bonds
Answer. (*c*)
249. The bond angles associated with the hybrid orbitals of a carbon involved in a triple bond is
(*a*) 180°

(*b*) 120°
(*c*) 109°
(*d*) 45°
Answer. (*a*)
250. How many electrons are involved in a carbon-carbon triple bond?
(*a*) 1
(*b*) 2
(*c*) 3
(*d*) 6
Answer. (*d*)
251. Which of the following *improperly* describes the physical properties of an alkyne?
(*a*) relatively nonpolar
(*b*) nearly insoluble in water
(*c*) less dense than water
(*d*) insoluble in most organic solvents
Answer. (*d*)
252. Which of the following statements correctly describes the general reactivity of alkynes?
(*a*) An alkyne is an electron-rich molecule and therefore reacts as a nucleophile.
(*b*) The σ bonds of alkynes are higher in energy than the bonds and are thus more reactive.
(*c*) Unlike alkenes, alkynes fail to undergo electrophilic addition reactions.
(*d*) Alkynes are generally more reactive than alkenes.
Answer. (*d*)
253. Which of the following describes a triple bond?
(*a*) two *sigma* bonds and two *pi* bonds
(*b*) one *sigma* bond and one *pi* bond
(*c*) two *sigma* bonds and one *pi* bond
(*d*) one *sigma* bond and two *pi* bonds
Answer. (*d*)
254. What two atomic orbitals or hybrid atomic orbitals overlap to form the carbon-carbon σ bond in ethyne?

(*a*) sp^3–sp^3
(*b*) sp^2–sp^2
(*c*) *s*–*s*
(*d*) *sp*–*sp*
Answer. (*d*)
255. Which of the following statements is *not* true about propyne, HC–C≡CH_3?
(*a*) It contains six *sigma* bonds.
(*b*) It contains three *pi* bonds.
(*c*) The H–C–H bond angle is about 109.5°.
(*d*) The C–C–C bond angle is 180°.
Answer. (*b*)
256. How many distinct terminal alkynes exist with a molecular formula of C_5H_8?
(*a*) 1
(*b*) 2
(*c*) 3
(*d*) 4
Answer. (*b*)
257. How many distinct internal alkynes exist with a molecular formula of C_6H_{10}?
(*a*) 1
(*b*) 2
(*c*) 3
(*d*) 4
Answer. (*c*)
258. Which is the correct order of decreasing acidity in the following compounds?
A. H_2O B. CH_3CH_3 C. NH_3 D. $CH_2=CH_2$ E. HC≡CH
(*a*) A > E > C > D > B
(*b*) A > E > D > B > C
(*c*) E > A > C > B > D
(*d*) A > C > E > D > B
Answer. (*a*)

259. Which of the following compounds is the major product when 1-hexyne is treated with excess HBr?
(*a*) 1,1-dibromohexane
(*b*) 1,1-dibromohexene
(*c*) 1,2-dibromohexene
(*d*) 2,2-dibromohexane
Answer. (*d*)
260. The reagent needed to convert 2-butyne to *cis*-2-butene is :
(*a*) H_2/Pt
(*b*) H_2/Lindlar's catalyst
(*c*) Li/NH_3
(*d*) Na/NH_3
Answer. (*b*)
261. Among the compounds water, 1-butyne, 2-butyne, and ethane, which are stronger acids than ammonia?
(*a*) 1-butyne and ethane
(*b*) water and 1-butyne
(*c*) water and ethane
(*d*) 1-butyne and 2-butyne
Answer. (*b*)
262. What is the product when 3-heptyne reacts with the Lindlar catalyst?
(*a*) 2-methyl-2-heptene
(*b*) *trans*-3-heptene
(*c*) *cis*-2-methyl-3-hexene
(*d*) *cis*-3-hexene
Answer. (*d*)
263. In the addition of hydrogen bromide to alkynes, which of the following species is believed to be an intermediate?
(*a*) vinyl anion
(*b*) vinyl cation
(*c*) vinyl radical
(*d*) carbene
Answer. (*b*)

264. Starting with 2-butene, which of the following is the best method for preparing
2-butyne?
(*a*) HBr; H_2/Ni; Zn/H+
(*b*) HBr; Zn/H+; H_2/Ni
(*c*) Br2/CCl_4; Zn/H^+; H_2/Ni
(*d*) Br_2/CCl_4; 2$NaNH_2$
Answer. (*d*)
265. In the following hydrogenation reactions ;

$$HC\equiv CH \xrightarrow{H_2/Ni} CH_2=CH_2 \xrightarrow{H_2/Ni} CH_3CH_3$$

The hybrid state of the carbon atom changes from
(*a*) $sp^3 \rightarrow sp^2 \rightarrow sp$
(*b*) $sp \rightarrow sp^2 \rightarrow sp^3$
(*c*) $sp^2 \rightarrow sp^3 \rightarrow sp$
(*d*) $sp^3 \rightarrow sp \rightarrow sp^2$
Answer. (*b*)
266. Which of the following hydrocarbons has acidic hydrogens?
(*a*) 1-Butene
(*b*) 1-Butyne
(*c*) 2-Butene
(*d*) 2-Butyne
Answer. (*b*)
267. Lindlar's catalyst is
(*a*) $LiAlH_4$
(*b*) Pd/$BaSO_4$ in Quinoline
(*c*) NH_2NH_2
(*d*) HCl/$ZnCl_2$
Answer. (*b*)
268. The higher reactivity of an alkene or alkyne, as compared to an alkane, is due to
(*a*) *sigma* bonds
(*b*) *pi* bonds
(*c*) hydrogen bonds
(*d*) None of these

Answer. (*b*)

269. Which of the following statements about alkenes and alkynes is correct?

(*a*) Alkynes are reduced *more* readily than alkenes.

(*b*) Alkynes are reduced *less* readily than alkenes.

(*c*) Alkynes and alkenes are reduced with *equal* speed.

(*d*) Alkynes and alkenes can not be reduced.

Answer. (*a*)

270. Which of the following sequences regarding acid-strength is correct?

(*a*) $HC\equiv CH > CH_3CH_2OH > CH_3COOH$

(*b*) $HC\equiv CH > CH_3COOH > CH_3CH_2OH$

(*c*) $CH_3COOH > HC\equiv CH > CH_3CH_2OH$

(*d*) $CH_3COOH > CH_3CH_2OH > HC\equiv CH$

Answer. (*d*)

271. 1,2-Dichloroethane reacts with excess of $NaNH_2$ to form

(*a*) Vinyl chloride

(*b*) Ethylene

(*c*) Ethyl chloride

(*d*) Acetylene

Answer. (*d*)

272. Propyne is formed by

(*a*) Polymerization of acetylene

(*b*) Reaction of acetylene with methane

(*c*) Reaction of acetylene with methyl chloride

(*d*) Reaction of sodium acetylide with methyl chloride

Answer. (*d*)

273. Which of the following compounds on hydrolysis gives acetylene?

(*a*) CaC_2

(*b*) Mg_2C_3

(*c*) Al_4C_3

(*d*) Cu_2Cl_2

Answer. (*a*)

274. Which of the following compounds on hydrolysis gives propyne?
(*a*) CaC_2
(*b*) Mg_2C_3
(*c*) Al_4C_3
(*d*) Cu_2Cl_2
Answer. (*c*)
275. Which one of the following compounds will (*a*) decolorizes dilute cold $KMnO_4$; (*b*) decolorizes bromine water ; and (*c*) gives a white precipitate with ammoniacal $AgNO_3$ solution.
(*a*) 1-Hexene
(*b*) 1-Hexyne
(*c*) 2-Hexene
(*d*) 2-Hexyne
Answer. (*b*)
276. Ethylene and acetylene can be distinguished by using
(*a*) Bromine in CCl_4
(*b*) Tollens' reagent
(*b*) Baeyer's reagent
(*d*) Phenylhydrazine
Answer. (*b*)
277. 1-Butyne can be distinguished from 2-butyne by using
(*a*) potassium permanganate
(*b*) bromine in CCl_4
(*c*) Tollens' reagent
(*d*) chlorine in CCl_4
Answer. (*c*)
278. 1-Butyne reacts with
(*a*) $NaNH_2$
(*b*) Dil H_2SO_4 and $HgSO_4$
(*c*) HBr
(*d*) All of these
Answer. (*d*)
279. Propyne can be converted to propene by using
(*a*) H_2 + Lindlar's catalyst

(*b*) NH_2NH_2
(*c*) H_2 + Pt catalyst
(*d*) NH_2NH_2 + KOH
Answer. (*a*)
280. 2-Butyne undergoes catalytic hydrogenation in the presence of Lindlar's catalyst to give
(*a*) 2-Butene
(*b*) Butane
(*c*) 1-Butene
(*d*) 2-Methylpropene
Answer. (*a*)
281. Addition of two moles of HCl to propyne gives :
(*a*) 2,2-Dichloropropane
(*b*) 1,3-Dichloropropane
(*c*) 1,2-Dichloropropane
(*d*) None of these
Answer. (*a*)
282. Propyne reacts with aqueous H_2SO_4 in the presence of $HgSO_4$ to form
(*a*) acetone
(*b*) 1-propanol
(*c*) acetaldehyde
(*d*) 2-propanol
Answer. (*a*)
283. Acetylene reacts with water in the presence of sulfuric acid and mercuric sulfate to give
(*a*) Acetone
(*b*) Acetic acid
(*c*) Formaldehyde
(*d*) Acetaldehyde
Answer. (*d*)
284. Which of the following compounds will react with ammoniacal silver nitrate?
(*a*) 1-Butene
(*b*) 1-Butyne
(*c*) 2-Butene

(*d*) 2-Butyne
Answer. (*b*)
285. Which of the following compounds does not react with ammoniacal $AgNO_3$ solution?
(*a*) Acetylene
(*b*) 1-Butyne
(*c*) Propyne
(*d*) 2-Butyne
Answer. (*d*)
286. Which of the following compounds reacts with ammoniacal cuprous chloride to give a precipitate?
(*a*) 1-Butene
(*b*) 1-Butyne
(*c*) 2-Butene
(*d*) 2-Butyne
Answer. (*b*)
287. Ozonolysis of 2-butyne gives
(*a*) Formic acid
(*b*) Propanoic acid
(*c*) Acetic acid
(*d*) Butanoic acid
Answer. (*c*)
288. Which alkyne yields propanoic acid as the only product upon treatment with ozone followed by hydrolysis?
(*a*) 1-Butyne
(*b*) 2-Hexyne
(*c*) 1-Pentyne
(*d*) 3-Hexyne
Answer. (*d*)
289. When acetylene is passed through hot iron tube at 400°C, it gives
(*a*) Benzene
(*b*) Toluene
(*c*) *o*-Xylene
(*d*) Mesitylene
Answer. (*a*)

290. When propyne is passed through hot iron tube at 400°C, it gives
(*a*) Benzene
(*b*) Toluene
(*c*) *m*-Xylene
(*d*) Mesitylene
Answer. (*d*)
291. The monomer for Neoprene is
(*a*) Isoprene
(*b*) acrylonitrile
(*c*) Chloroprene
(*d*) 1,3-butadiene
Answer. (*c*)
292. A compound, C_4H_6, reacts with bromine and forms a white precipitate with ammoniacal silver nitrate solution. It reacts with dilute H_2SO_4 in the presence of mercuric sulfate to form 2-butanone. The compound could be
(*a*) 1-Butyne
(*b*) 1-Butene
(*c*) 2-Butyne
(*d*) 2-Butene
Answer. (*a*)
293. Which of the following correctly ranks the cycloalkanes in order of increasing ring strain per methylene?
(*a*) cyclopropane < cyclobutane < cyclohexane < cycloheptane
(*b*) cyclohexane < cyclopentane < cyclobutane < cyclopropane
(*c*) cyclopentane < cyclobutane < cyclopentane < cyclopropane
(*d*) cyclopentane < cyclopropane < cyclobutane < cyclohexane
Answer. (*b*)
294. Which of the following has two equatorial alkyl substituents in its most stable conformation?
(*a*) 1,1-dimethylcyclohexane

(*b*) *cis*-1,2-dimethylcyclohexane
(*c*) *cis*-1,3-diethylcyclohexane
(*d*) *cis*-1,4-diethylcyclohexane
Answer. (*c*)
295. Which one of the following is not a metal catalyst for the hydrogenation of an alkene?
(*a*) Pd
(*b*) Pt
(*c*) Na
(*d*) Ni
Answer. (*c*)
296. What is(are) the product(s) in the Pd-catalyzed hydrogenation of 1,2-dimethylcyclopentene?
(*a*) *trans*-1,2-dimethylcyclopentane
(*b*) *cis*-1,2-dimethylcyclopentane
(*c*) a mixture of *trans* and *cis*-1,2-dimethylcyclopentane
(*d*) 1,1-dimethylcyclopentane
Answer. (*b*)
297. Which of the following is not a possible reaction of a carbocation?
(*a*) addition of a nucleophile
(*b*) rearrangement to a more stable carbocation
(*c*) addition of a proton to form an alkane
(*d*) loss of a β-hydrogen to form an alkene
Answer. (*c*)
298. Addition of HCl to 3-methyl-1-pentene gives two products. One of these is 2-chloro-3-methylpentane. What is the other product?
(*a*) 1-Chloro-3-methylpentane
(*b*) 3-Chloro-3-methylpentane
(*c*) 3-Chloro-2-methylpentane
(*d*) 2-Chloro-2-methylpentane
Answer. (*b*)
299. Predict which of the following alkenes reacts the fastest with HCl?
(*a*) $CH_3CH_2CH_2CH_2CH=CH_2$

(*b*) *cis*-$CH_3CH_2CH=CHCH_2CH_3$
(*c*) *trans*-$CH_3CH_2CH=CHCH_2CH_3$
(*d*) $(CH_3)_2C=CHCH_2CH_3$
Answer. (*d*)
300. The hydroboration-oxidation reaction can be characterized as the _________ to an alkene.
(*a*) *anti*-Markovnikov *syn* addition of water
(*b*) *anti*-Markovnikov *anti* addition of water
(*c*) Markovnikov *syn* addition of water
(*d*) Markovnikov *anti* addition of water
Answer. (*a*)
301. A compound, $C_{15}H_{24}$, is reacted with excess hydrogen using a metal catalyst. One equivalent of the compound consumed three equivalents of hydrogen. How many rings did the original compound have?
(*a*) 1 only
(*b*) 2 only
(*c*) 3 only
(*d*) None of these
Answer. (*a*)
302. The reaction of 1-butene with bromine, Br_2, in aqueous solution gives primarily
1-bromo-2-butanol. Identify the nucleophilic species in the reaction.
(*a*) Br_2
(*b*) Br^-
(*c*) H_2O
(*d*) HOBr
Answer. (*c*)
303. Which brief statement most accurately describes why alkenes react the way they do?
(*a*) C=C double bonds are weak.
(*b*) A π bond is lost but a stronger σ bond is gained.
(*c*) C=C double bonds are unstable.
(*d*) C=C π bonds are attacked by nucleophiles.
Answer. (*b*)

304. Which of the following poisonous gas is formed when chloroform is exposed to light and air?
(*a*) Mustard gas
(*b*) Carbon monoxide
(*c*) Phosgene
(*d*) Chlorine
Answer. (*c*)
305. Freon-12, CCl_2F_2, is used as a
(*a*) Local anesthetic
(*b*) Dry-cleaning agent
(*c*) Refrigerant
(*d*) Disinfectant
Answer. (*c*)
306. Which of the following compounds has been suggested as causing depletion of the ozone layer in the upper stratosphere?
(*a*) CH_4
(*b*) CCl_2F_2
(*c*) CF_4
(*d*) CH_2Cl_2
Answer. (*b*)
307. Which of the following reagents cannot be used to prepare an alkyl chloride from an alcohol?
(*a*) $HCl + ZnCl_2$
(*b*) $SOCl_2$
(*c*) $NaCl$
(*d*) PCl_5
Answer. (*c*)
308. 2-Propanol reacts with KBr and concentrated H_2SO_4 to give
(*a*) 1-Bromopropane
(*b*) 1,2-Dibromopropane
(*c*) 2-Bromopropane
(*d*) 2,2-Dibromopropane
Answer. (*c*)

309. The best way to prepare 1,2-Dibromoethane is to treat :
(*a*) Ethylene with Br_2
(*b*) Acetylene with excess of HBr
(*c*) Ethylene with excess of HBr
(*d*) 1,2-Dichloroethane with Br_2
Answer. (*a*)
310. Alkyl halides undergo
(*a*) Electrophilic substitution reactions
(*b*) Electrophilic addition reactions
(*c*) Nucleophilic substitution reactions
(*d*) Nucleophilic addition reactions
Answer. (*c*)
311. *n*-Propyl iodide reacts with sodium ethoxide to give :
(*a*) $CH_3CH_2OCH_2CH_3$
(*b*) $CH_3CH_2OCH_2CH_2CH_3$
(*c*) $CH_3CH_2OCH_3$
(*d*) $CH_3OCH_2CH_2CH_3$
Answer. (*b*)
312. 1-Bromobutane reacts with alcoholic KOH to mainly give
(*a*) 1-Butene
(*b*) 2-Butene
(*c*) 1-Butanol
(*d*) 2-Butanol
Answer. (*b*)
313. 2-Bromobutane reacts alcoholic KOH to mainly give
(*a*) 1-Butene
(*b*) 2-Butene
(*c*) 1-Butanol
(*d*) 2-Butanol
Answer. (*b*)
314. Isopropyl bromide reacts with alcoholic KOH to give
(*a*) Propene
(*b*) Isopropyl alcohol
(*c*) Propane

(*d*) *n*-Propyl alcohol
Answer. (*a*)
315. 2,2-Dichloropropane reacts with aqueous KOH to give
(*a*) 2,2-Propanediol
(*b*) Propanal
(*c*) Acetone
(*d*) Propene
Answer. (*c*)

$$CH_3-\underset{Cl}{\overset{Cl}{C}}-CH_3 \xrightarrow{\text{aq KOH}} \left[CH_3-\underset{OH}{\overset{OH}{C}}-CH_3\right] \xrightarrow{-H_2O} CH_3-\overset{O}{\overset{\|}{C}}-CH_3$$

2,2-Dichloropropane — Unstable — Acetone

316. 1,1-Dichloropropane reacts with aqueous KOH to give
(*a*) 1,1-Propanediol
(*b*) Acetaldehyde
(*c*) Propanone
(*d*) Propyne
Answer. (*b*)
317. Which of the following compounds will not give a white precipitate with alcoholic $AgNO_3$.
(*a*) Bromobenzene
(*b*) 1-Bromopropane
(*c*) Ethyl bromide
(*d*) 2-Bromopropane
Answer. (*a*)
318. Which of the following compounds will give a white precipitate with alcoholic $AgNO_3$?
(*a*) Vinylbenzene
(*b*) Chlorobenzene
(*c*) Vinyl chloride
(*d*) Allyl chloride
Answer. (*d*)
319. Carbylamine test involves heating a mixture of
(*a*) alcoholic KOH, methyl iodide, and sodium metal
(*b*) alcoholic KOH, methyl iodide, and primary amine

(*c*) alcoholic KOH, chloroform, and primary amine
(*d*) alcoholic KOH, methyl alcohol, and primary amine
Answer. (*c*)
320. When chloroform is heated with aqueous NaOH, it gives
(*a*) Formic acid
(*b*) Sodium formate
(*c*) Acetic acid
(*d*) Sodium acetate
Answer. (*b*)
321. Which alkyl halides react most readily by nucleophilic substitution?
(*a*) CH_3CH_2Cl
(*b*) CH_3CH_2I
(*c*) CH_3CH_2Br
(*d*) CH_3CH_2F
Answer. (*b*)
322. Which of the following factors influence whether a reaction will proceed by an S_N1, S_N2, E1, or E2 mechanism?
(*a*) Structure of the alkyl halide
(*b*) Solvent
(*c*) Concentration of reagents
(*d*) Nature of the nucleophile
(*e*) All of these
Answer. (*e*)
323. Which compound reacts most rapidly by an S_N1 mechanism?
(*a*) Methyl chloride
(*b*) Isopropyl chloride
(*c*) Ethyl chloride
(*d*) *tert*-Butyl chloride
Answer. (*d*)
324. Which of the following compounds would react most rapidly in an S_N2 reaction?
(*a*) CH_3CH_2I
(*b*) $CH_2{=}CH{-}I$

(*c*) $(CH_3)_2CHI$
(*d*) $(CH_3)_3CI$
Answer. (*a*)
325. There are 8 isomers that have the molecular formula $C_5H_{11}Br$. How many of these are tertiary alkyl bromides?
(*a*) 1
(*b*) 2
(*c*) 3
(*d*) 8
Answer. (*a*)
326. Which of the following statements is correct for a saturated alkyl halide?
(*a*) the C–X bond results from overlap of the *s* orbital of carbon and the *p* orbital of the halogen (X)
(*b*) the C–X bond results from overlap of the *p* orbital of carbon and the *p* orbital of the halogen (X)
(*c*) the C–X bond results from overlap of the sp^3 orbital of carbon and the *p* orbital of the halogen (X)
(*d*) the C–X bond results from overlap of the sp^2 orbital of carbon and the *p* orbital of the halogen (X)
Answer. (*c*)
327. Which of the following best describes the carbon-chlorine bond of an alkyl chloride?
(*a*) nonpolar; no dipole
(*b*) polar; δ+ at carbon and δ– at chlorine
(*c*) polar; δ– at carbon and δ+ at chlorine
(*d*) ionic
Answer. (*b*)
328. Which of the following is a secondary alkyl halide?
(*a*) CH_3Br
(*b*) $(CH_3)_3CBr$
(*c*) $(CH_3)_2CHBr$
(*d*) $(CH_3)_2CHCH_2Br$
Answer. (*c*)
329. How should $CH_3CHClCH_2CH_3$ be classified?
(*a*) primary alkyl halide

(*b*) secondary alkyl halide
(*c*) tertiary alkyl halide
(*d*) quarternary alkyl halide
Answer. (*b*)
330. Which of the following will have the lowest boiling point?
(*a*) CH_3Cl
(*b*) CH_4
(*c*) CH_2Cl_2
(*d*) $CHCl_3$
Answer. (*b*)
331. Which of the following is *not* correct concerning substitution and elimination reactions of alkyl halides?
(*a*) The electrophile replaces the leaving group.
(*b*) Compounds containing electron-donating groups bonded to an sp^3 hybridized carbon undergo substitution and elimination reactions.
(*c*) The electronegative atom is replaced by another atom or group in substitution reactions.
(*d*) (*a*) and (*b*)
Answer. (*d*)
332. Which of the following statements concerning S_N2 reactions of alkyl halides is *not* correct?
(*a*) The rate of reaction depends on the concentration of the nucleophile.
(*b*) The rate of reaction depends on the concentration of the alkyl halide.
(*c*) The rate of reaction of a particular alkyl bromide depends on the steric accessibility of the carbon of the C-Br bond.
(*d*) All alkyl iodides react more rapidly than all alkyl chlorides.
Answer. (*d*)
333. Which of the following correctly reflects relative stabilities of carbocations?
(*a*) 3° allylic > 2° > 1° benzylic

(*b*) methyl > 2° benzylic > 3°
(*c*) 3° benzylic > vinyl > 1°
(*d*) 2° allylic > 2° > vinyl
Answer. (*d*)
334. Which of the following species is most reactive in a S_N2 reaction?
(*a*) CH_3CH_2Cl
(*b*) CH_3CH_2Br
(*c*) CH_3CH_2I
(*d*) CH_3CH_2F
Answer. (*c*)
335. Which of the following is the best leaving group?
(*a*) F^-
(*b*) Cl^-
(*c*) Br^-
(*d*) I^-
Answer. (*d*)
336. Which of the following is the strongest nucleophile in an aqueous solution?
(*a*) HO^-
(*b*) Cl^-
(*c*) Br^-
(*d*) I^-
Answer. (*d*)
337. Which of the following is the best nucleophile in water?
(*a*) I^-
(*b*) CH_3SCH_3
(*c*) CH_3OCH_3
(*d*) Cl^-
Answer. (*a*)
338. Which of the following compounds will undergo an S_N2 reaction most readily?
(*a*) $(CH_3)_3CCH_2I$
(*b*) $(CH_3)_3CCl$
(*c*) $(CH_3)_2CHI$
(*d*) $(CH_3)_2CHCH_2CH_2CH_2I$

Answer. (*d*)

339. Which of the following is the rate law for S_N1 mechanisms?

(*a*) Rate = k[Alkyl Halide] [Nucleophile]
(*b*) Rate = k[Nucleophile]
(*c*) Rate = k[Alkyl Halide]
(*d*) Rate = k_1[Alkyl Halide] + k_2[Nucleophile]

Answer. (*c*)

340. Which of the following factors has *no* effect on the rate of S_N1 reactions?

(*a*) the nature of the alkyl halide
(*b*) the nature of the leaving group
(*c*) the concentration of the alkyl halide
(*d*) the concentration of the nucleophile

Answer. (*d*)

341. Which is the most reactive alkyl halide in a S_N1 reaction?

(*a*) CH_3F
(*b*) CH_3Br
(*c*) CH_3I
(*d*) CH_3Cl

Answer. (*c*)

342. Which of the following halides is most reactive in an E2 reaction with sodium
methoxide?

(*a*) $(CH_3)_3CCH_2I$
(*b*) $(CH_3)_2CHCHICH_3$
(*c*) $(CH_3)_2CHCH_2Br$
(*d*) $(CH_3)_2CHCH_2Cl$

Answer. (*b*)

343. Which of the following halides is *least* reactive in an E2 reaction with sodium methoxide?

(*a*) $(CH_3)_3CCH_2I$
(*b*) $(CH_3)_2CHCHICH_3$
(*c*) $(CH_3)_2CHCH_2Br$
(*d*) $(CH_3)_2CHCH_2Cl$

Answer. (*a*)
344. Dehydrohalogenation of 2-bromobutane in the presence of a strong base proceeds *via* which of the following mechanistic pathways?
(*a*) S_N1
(*b*) S_N2
(*c*) E1
(*d*) E2
Answer. (*d*)
345. Which of the alkyl chlorides listed below undergoes dehydrohalogenation in the presence of a strong base to give 2-pentene as the only alkene product?
(*a*) 1-chloropentane
(*b*) 2-chloropentane
(*c*) 3-chloropentane
(*d*) 1-chloro-2-methylbutane
Answer. (*c*)
346. Predict the two most likely mechanisms for the reaction of 2-iodohexane with sodium ethoxide.
(*a*) S_N2 and S_N1
(*b*) E1 and E2
(*c*) S_N2 and E2
(*d*) E1 and S_N1
Answer. (*c*)
347. Predict the two most likely mechanisms which occur when 2-iodohexane is heated in ethanol.
(*a*) S_N2 and S_N1
(*b*) E1 and E2
(*c*) S_N2 and E2
(*d*) E1 and S_N1
Answer. (*d*)
348. Grignard reagents do not show any reaction with
(*a*) Alkoxyalkanes
(*b*) Alkanones
(*c*) Alkyl alkanoates
(*d*) Acyl halides

Answer. (*a*)

349. The Grignard reagent, CH_3CH_2MgBr, can be used to prepare

(*a*) Ethane

(*b*) 3-Ethyl-3-pentanol

(*c*) Propanoic acid

(*d*) All of these

Answer. (*d*)

350. Which is the best reagent to accomplish the following conversion?

$$CH_3CH_2Br \xrightarrow{(?)} CH_3CH_3$$

(*a*) Conc. H_2SO_4

(*b*) Na

(*c*) Conc. HCl

(*d*) Mg, then H_2O

Answer. (*d*)

351. What is the major product of the following reaction?

$$CH_3CH_2-\overset{\overset{\large O}{\|}}{C}-H \ + \ CH_3MgBr \longrightarrow \ \xrightarrow{H_2O/H^+}$$

(*a*) 1-Butanol

(*b*) Butanal

(*c*) 2-Butanol

(*d*) Butanone

Answer. (*c*)

352. Ethylmagnesium iodide reacts with formaldehyde to give a product which on acid-hydrolysis forms :

(*a*) an aldehyde

(*b*) a primary alcohol

(*c*) a ketone

(*d*) a secondary alcohol

Answer. (*b*)

353. Ketones react with Grignard reagents to form an addition product which on hydrolysis gives a

(*a*) Primary alcohol

(*b*) Tertiary alcohol

(*c*) Secondary alcohol
(*d*) Ketal
Answer. (*b*)
354. *n*-Propylmagnesium bromide on treatment with carbon dioxide and further hydrolysis gives :
(*a*) Acetic acid
(*b*) Propanoic acid
(*c*) Butanoic acid
(*d*) Formic acid
Answer. (*c*)
355. Which of the following compounds will react with methylmagnesium iodide followed by acid-hydrolysis to give ethyl alcohol?
(*a*) Ethylene
(*b*) Acetaldehyde
(*c*) Formaldehyde
(*d*) Acetone
Answer. (*c*)
356. Which of the following gives a tertiary alcohol when treated with Grignard reagents?
(*a*) $H-\overset{\overset{O}{\|}}{C}-H$
(*b*) $CH_3-\overset{\overset{O}{\|}}{C}-H$
(*c*) $CH_3-\overset{\overset{O}{\|}}{C}-CH_3$
(*d*) None of these
Answer. (*c*)
357. Which of the following compounds will react with methylmagnesium bromide to give *tert*-butyl alcohol?
(*a*) Acetyl chloride
(*b*) Acetone
(*c*) Isopropyl alcohol
(*d*) Acetaldehyde
Answer. (*b*)

358. Phenylmagnesium bromide reacts with acetaldehyde to form an addition product which undergoes acid-hydrolysis to give
(*a*) Diphenylcarbinol
(*b*) Benzyl alcohol
(*c*) Methylphenylcarbinol
(*d*) Benzoic acid
Answer. (*c*)
359. Which of the following is the strongest base?
(*a*) HOMgBr
(*b*) H_2O
(*c*) CH_3OH
(*d*) CH_3MgBr
Answer. (*d*)
360. Which of the following is correct?
(*a*) When a Grignard reagent reacts with a ketone, the addition product is a primary alcohol.
(*b*) When a Grignard reagent reacts with a ketone, the addition product is a secondary alcohol.
(*c*) When a Grignard reagent reacts with a aldehyde, the addition product is a tertiary alcohol.
(*d*) None of the above are correct.
Answer. (*d*)
361. Which of the following alcohols can be prepared by the reaction of methyl formate with excess Grignard reagent?
(*a*) 1-pentanol
(*b*) 2-pentanol
(*c*) 3-pentanol
(*d*) 2-methyl-2-pentanol
Answer. (*c*)
362. The number of structural isomers of alcohols with molecular formula C_3H_7OH is
(*a*) 5
(*b*) 4
(*c*) 3
(*d*) 2

Answer. (*d*)

363. The number of structural isomers of alcohols with molecular formula C_4H_9OH is

(*a*) 5

(*b*) 4

(*c*) 3

(*d*) 6

Answer. (*b*)

364. Why do alcohols have boiling points much higher than hydrocarbons of similar molecular weight?

(*a*) Alcohols have greater van der Waals attraction forces.

(*b*) Alcohol molecules have greater molecular symmetry.

(*c*) Hydrogen bonds must be broken in the process of volatilization.

(*d*) Alcohols must overcome greater ionic forces in the process of volatilization.

Answer. (*c*)

365. The high boiling points of alcohols, as compared to the corresponding alkanes, are due to

(*a*) Hydrogen bonding

(*b*) Heavy oxygen atom

(*c*) Water solubility

(*d*) None of these

Answer. (*a*)

366. Which of the following has the highest boiling point?

(*a*) diethyl ether

(*b*) *n*-Butyraldehyde

(*c*) *n*-propyl chloride

(*d*) *n*-Butyl alcohol

Answer. (*d*)

367. Which of the following has the highest boiling point?

(*a*) $CH_3CH_2CH_2CH_2Cl$

(*b*) $HOCH_2CH_2CH_2CH_2OH$

(*c*) $CH_3CH_2CH_2CH_2OH$

(*d*) $CH_3CH_2OCH_2CH_3$

Answer. (*b*)

368. Which of the following compounds has the highest boiling point?

(*a*) $CH_3CH_2-\overset{\overset{\large O}{\|}}{C}-H$

(*b*) $CH_3CH_2CH_2OH$

(*c*) $CH_3-\overset{\overset{\large O}{\|}}{C}-CH_3$

(*d*) $CH_3CH_2OCH_3$

Answer. (*b*)

369. Which of the following has the highest boiling point?

(*a*) CH_3CH_2OH

(*b*) $CH_3CH_2CH_2CH_2OH$

(*c*) CH_3OH

(*d*) $CH_3CH_2CH_2OH$

Answer. (*b*)

370. Rank the following substances in order of increasing boiling point (lowest → highest):

(1) $CH_3CH_2CH_2CH_2OH$, (2) $(CH_3)_2CHOCH_3$, (3) $(CH_3)_3COH$

(*a*) (1) < (2) < (3)

(*b*) (2) < (1) < (3)

(*c*) (2) < (3) < (1)

(*d*) (3) < (2) < (1)

Answer. (*c*)

371. Which of the following compounds is the least soluble in water?

(*a*) $HOCH_2CH_2OH$

(*b*) $CH_3CH_2CH_2OH$

(*c*) CH_3CH_2OH

(*d*) $CH_3CH_2CH_2CH_2OH$

Answer. (*d*)

372. Methanol is known as :

(*a*) Rubbing alcohol

(*b*) Grain alcohol

(*c*) Wood alcohol

(*d*) Denatured alcohol

Answer. (*c*)
373. Rectified spirit is
(*a*) 100% Ethanol
(*b*) 90% Ethanol
(*c*) 100% Methanol
(*d*) 95% Ethanol
Answer. (*d*)
374. Grain alcohol is another name for
(*a*) Methyl alcohol
(*b*) Isopropyl alcohol
(*c*) Ethyl alcohol
(*d*) *n*-Propyl alcohol
Answer. (*c*)
375. Lucas reagents is
(*a*) $HCl/NaNO_2$
(*b*) H_2/Pd
(*c*) $HCl/ZnCl_2$
(*d*) $H_2/Pd/BaSO_4$
Answer. (*c*)
376. Lucas test is used to determine the type of
(*a*) alcohols
(*b*) acids
(*c*) amines
(*d*) carbohydrates
Answer. (*a*)
377. Which of the following gives positive Iodoform test :
(*a*) 1-Propanol
(*b*) 2-Propanol
(*c*) 3-Propanol
(*d*) None of these
Answer. (*b*)
378. Which of the following reagents will replace –OH group by a halogen atom?
(*a*) HOCl
(*b*) Br_2
(*c*) $SOCl_2$

(*d*) I_2
Answer. (*c*)
379. The compound which reacts most readily with Lucas reagent is
(*a*) CH_3CH_2Cl
(*b*) $(CH_3)_2CHOH$
(*c*) CH_3CH_2OH
(*d*) $(CH_3)_3COH$
Answer. (*d*)
380. Which of the following compounds reacts slowest with Lucas reagent at room temperature?
(*a*) 1-butanol
(*b*) 2-propanol
(*c*) 2-butanol
(*d*) 2-methyl-2-propanol
Answer. (*a*)
381. Which of the following compounds will react fastest with Lucas reagent?
(*a*) 1-propanol
(*b*) 2-methyl-1-propanol
(*c*) 2-propanol
(*d*) 2-methyl-2-propanol
Answer. (*d*)
382. Which of the following compounds reacts fastest with HBr?
(*a*) 1-propanol
(*b*) 2-methyl-1-propanol
(*c*) 2-propanol
(*d*) 2-methyl-2-propanol
Answer. (*d*)
383. When ethanol is treated with sodium metal :
(*a*) Sodium ethoxide is formed
(*b*) The sodium is oxidized
(*c*) The acidic hydrogen in reduced
(*d*) All these occur
Answer. (*d*)

384. Which of the following alcohols will give a yellow precipitate of iodoform with iodine and dilute NaOH solution?
(*a*) 1-Propanol
(*b*) 2-Propanol
(*c*) 1-Butanol
(*d*) 2-Methyl-2-propanol
Answer. (*b*)
385. Ethyl alcohol can react with concentrated H_2SO_4 to give
(*a*) Ethylene
(*b*) Diethyl ether
(*c*) Ethyl hydrogen sulfate
(*d*) All of these
Answer. (*d*)
386. Ethanol on heating with concentrated H_2SO_4 at 170°C gives
(*a*) ethylene
(*b*) ethyl hydrogen sulfate
(*c*) diethyl ether
(*d*) diethyl sulfate
Answer. (*a*)
387. The major product of acid-catalyzed dehydration of 2-butanol is :
(*a*) 2-Butene
(*b*) 2-Butyne
(*c*) 1-Butene
(*d*) 1-Butyne
Answer. (*a*)
388. Which is the best reagent for carrying out the following conversion?

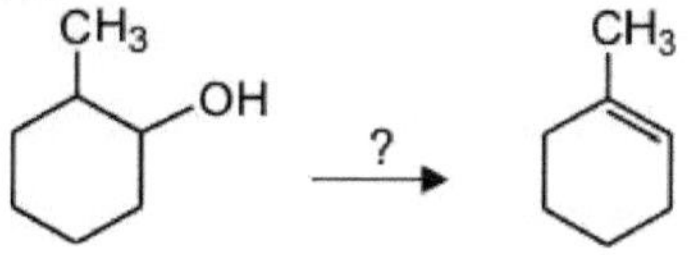

CH3 OH ? CH3

(*a*) $LiAlH_4$

(*b*) Conc H_2SO_4
(*c*) H_2/Ni
(*d*) NaOH
Answer. (*b*)
389. Which of the following reaction mixtures will give an organic product which is ionic?
(*a*) $CH_3CH_2OH + PCl_5$
(*b*) $CH_3CH_2OH + KBr + H_2SO_4$
(*c*) $CH_3CH_2OH + Na$
(*d*) $CH_3CH_2OH + SOCl_2$
Answer. (*c*)
390. Hydroboration-oxidation of propene gives :
(*a*) Isopropyl alcohol
(*b*) *n*-Propyl alcohol
(*c*) Isobutyl alcohol
(*d*) *tert*-Butyl alcohol
Answer. (*b*)
391. Hydroboration-oxidation of 2-Methylpropene gives
(*a*) 2-Methyl-2-propanol
(*b*) 1,2,3-Propanetriol
(*c*) 2-Methyl-1-propanol
(*d*) 1,2-Propanediol
Answer. (*c*)
392. Which of the following compounds will not be *easily* oxidized?
(*a*) Primary alcohol
(*b*) Secondary alcohol
(*c*) Tertiary alcohol
(*d*) Aldehyde
Answer. (*c*)
393. Which of the following is most resistant to oxidation?
(*a*) CH_3CH_2OH
(*b*) $(CH_3)_2CHOH$
(*c*) $HOCH_2CH_2OH$
(*d*) $(CH_3)_3COH$
Answer. (*d*)

394. Oxidation of a primary alcohol with produces
(*a*) a carboxylic acid
(*b*) an ether
(*c*) a ketone
(*d*) an ester
Answer. (*a*)
395. Oxidation of a secondary alcohol with $K_2Cr_2O_7/H^+$ produces
(*a*) a carboxylic acid
(*b*) a ketone
(*c*) an aldehyde
(*d*) an ester
Answer. (*b*)
396. Isopropyl alcohol reacts with acidic sodium dichromate to give
(*a*) Acetaldehyde
(*b*) Acetic acid
(*c*) Propionic acid
(*d*) Acetone
Answer. (*d*)
397. Isopropyl alcohol can be converted to acetone by treatment with
(*a*) $HCl/ZnCl_2$
(*b*) $Na_2Cr_2O_7/H_2SO_4$
(*c*) NaOH
(*d*) $LiAlH_4$
Answer. (*b*)
398. Which of the bonds in Ethyl alcohol (CH_3CH_2OH) will undergo heterolytic bond fission most readily?
(*a*) O–H
(*b*) C–H
(*c*) C–O
(*d*) C–C
Answer. (*a*)
399. The mechanism of dehydration of an alcohol to give an alkene involves formation of :

(*a*) Carbonium ions
(*b*) Carbanions
(*c*) Free radicals
(*d*) Carbenes
Answer. (*a*)
400. The mechanism of dehydration of an alcohol to give an ether involves formation of :
(*a*) Carbonium ions
(*b*) Carbanions
(*c*) Free radicals
(*d*) Carbenes
Answer. (*a*)
401. The acid-catalyzed dehydration mechanism for alcohols is best described as a(n) :
(*a*) E1
(*b*) E2
(*c*) S_N1
(*d*) S_N2
Answer. (*a*)
402. When ethanol is heated with concentrated H_2SO_4, a gas is produced. Which of the following compounds is formed when this gas is treated with bromine in CCl_4?E2
(*a*) Bromomethane
(*b*) 1,2-Dibromoethane
(*c*) Bromoethane
(*d*) 1,1,2,2-Tetrabromoethane
Answer. (*b*)
403. What is the functional group in an alcohol?
(*a*) Carbon-carbon double bond
(*b*) NH_2
(*c*) OH
(*d*) COOH
Answer. (*c*)
404. What is the IUPAC name for the following structure?
$CH_3CH(CH_3)CH_2CH(OH)CH_3$
(*a*) 4-methyl-2-pentanol

(*b*) 2-methyl-2-hexanol
(*c*) 2-methyl-4-pentanol
(*d*) 2-methyl-3-pentanol
Answer. (*a*)
405. Explain why the water molecule has a bent shape and a bond angle less than 109.5°.
Answer. The electron repulsion between the two lone pairs of electrons on the oxygen of water causes the O–H bonds to squeeze close together.
406. Which of the following compounds does *not* have the molecular formula $C_6H_{14}O$?
(*a*) 2-hexanol
(*b*) 3-methyl-2-pentanol
(*c*) 3-methyl-3-pentanol
(*d*) cyclohexanol
Answer. (*d*)
407. Which of the following is a secondary alcohol?
(*a*) 3-ethyl-2-methyl-1-pentanol
(*b*) 3-ethyl-2-methyl-2-heptanol
(*c*) 3-methyl-2-hexanol
(*d*) 1-hexanol
Answer. (*c*)
408. Which of the following is *sec*-butyl alcohol?
(*a*) $CH_3CH_2CH_2CH_2OH$
(*b*) $CH_3CH(OH)CH_2CH_3$
(*c*) $(CH_3)_2CHCH_2OH$
(*d*) $(CH_3)_2CHOH$
Answer. (*b*)
409. What is the hybridization of the oxygen atom in CH_3CH_2OH?
(*a*) *sp*
(*b*) 4sp^3
(*c*) sp^2
(*d*) sp^3
Answer. (*d*)

410. Where are the two lone pairs of electrons of the oxygen atom in an alcohol molecule located?
(*a*) in two *p* orbitals
(*b*) in two *sp* orbitals
(*c*) in two sp^2 orbitals
(*d*) in two sp^3 orbitals
Answer. (*d*)
411. What is the strongest intermolecular force present in liquid ethanol?
(*a*) induced dipole-induced dipole
(*b*) dipole-dipole, specifically hydrogen bonding
(*c*) dipole-dipole, but not hydrogen bonding
(*d*) ion-dipole
Answer. (*b*)
412. Which of the following is the best method for preparing CH_3Br?
(*a*) $CH_3OH + Br^-$
(*b*) $CH_3OH + HBr$
(*c*) $CH_3OH + Br_2$
(*d*) $CH_3OH + NaBr$
Answer. (*b*)
413. Which of the following reagents can be used to oxidize 1° alcohols to aldehydes?
(*a*) $KMnO_4$
(*b*) MnO_2
(*c*) $K_2Cr_2O_7$
(*d*) PCC
Answer. (*d*)
12. What is the major product from the acid-catalyzed hydration of 2-methyl-2-pentene?
(*a*) 2-methylpentane
(*b*) 2-methyl-1-pentanol
(*c*) 2-methyl-2-pentanol
(*d*) 2-methyl-3-pentanol
Answer. (*c*)

414. In cold countries ethylene glycol is added to water in car radiators. This helps to
(*a*) Reduce the viscosity
(*b*) Make water a better lubricant
(*c*) Lower the freezing point
(*d*) Lower the boiling point
Answer. (*c*)
415. Ethylene oxide undergoes acid-hydrolysis to form
(*a*) Ethylene glycol
(*b*) Formic acid
(*c*) Ethyl alcohol
(*d*) Acetic acid
Answer. (*a*)
416. Ethylene glycol undergoes oxidation with hot acidic $KMnO_4$ to form :
(*a*) Formic acid
(*b*) Formaldehyde
(*c*) Acetic acid
(*d*) Acetaldehyde
Answer. (*a*)
417. Ethylene glycol reacts with excess of PCl_5 to give
(*a*) Chloroethane
(*b*) 1,2-Dichloroethane
(*c*) Hexachloroethane
(*d*) 1,3-Dichloroethane
Answer. (*b*)
418. 1,2-Ethanediol reacts with anhydrous zinc chloride to form
(*a*) Ethylene
(*b*) Acetaldehyde
(*c*) Acetylene
(*d*) Ethyl chloride
Answer. (*b*)
419. When ethylene glycol is heated with concentrated HNO_3, it forms
(*a*) Oxalic acid

(*b*) Ethylene oxide
(*c*) Dioxane
(*d*) Diethylene glycol
Answer. (*a*)
420. Which of the following is used as an antifreeze?
(*a*) Ethylene glycol
(*b*) Glycerol
(*c*) Diethyl ether
(*d*) Picric acid
Answer. (*a*)
421. When glycerol is heated with oxalic acid at 260°C, it gives
(*a*) 1,2-Propanediol
(*b*) Vinyl alcohol
(*c*) 1,3-Propanediol
(*d*) Allyl alcohol
Answer. (*d*)
422. When glycerol is heated with potassium hydrogen sulfate ($KHSO_4$), it forms
(*a*) Acrolein
(*b*) Acetic acid
(*c*) Allyl alcohol
(*d*) Propionic acid
Answer. (*a*)
423. Glycerol on warming with a small amount of hydriodic acid gets converted to
(*a*) Propene
(*b*) 3-Iodopropene
(*c*) 1,3-Diiodopropane
(*d*) 2-Iodopropane
Answer. (*b*)
424. When glycerol is treated with a mixture of concentrated $HNO_3 + H_2SO_4$, it forms
(*a*) Nitroethane
(*b*) 1-Nitropropane
(*c*) Nitroglycerine

(*d*) 2-Nitropropane
Answer. (*c*)
425. In the manufacture of dynamite, one of the chemicals used is
(*a*) Glycerol
(*b*) Glycerol triacetate
(*c*) Glycerol trinitrate
(*d*) Glycerol triiodide
Answer. (*c*)
426. Which of the following compounds is least soluble in water?
(*a*) Glycerol
(*b*) Ethyl alcohol
(*c*) Ethylene glycol
(*d*) Ethyl chloride
Answer. (*d*)
427. Compound (A) reacts with sodium metal to form one mole of H_2. The compound (A) can be
(*a*) $CH_3CH_2CH=CH_2$
(*b*) $HOCH_2CH_2CH_2CH_2OH$
(*c*) $CH=CH-CH=CH_2$
(*d*) $CH_3CH_2CH_2CH_2OH$
Answer. (*b*)
428. Ethers are
(*a*) Lewis acids
(*b*) Neutral
(*c*) Lewis bases
(*d*) Can not be predicted
Answer. (*c*)
429. Ethanol is isomeric with
(*a*) Dimethyl ether
(*b*) Ethanal
(*c*) Diethyl ether
(*d*) Propanone
Answer. (*a*)
430. Diethyl ether and methyl propyl ether are

(*a*) Conformational isomers
(*b*) Metamers
(*c*) Geometrical isomers
(*d*) Enantiomers
Answer. (*b*)
431. The reaction of a sodium alkoxide with an alkyl halide is called
(*a*) Wurtz-Fittig reaction
(*b*) Perkin reaction
(*c*) Williamson's synthesis
(*d*) Aldol condensation
Answer. (*c*)
432. Ethyl bromide reacts with sodium methoxide to form
(*a*) Diethyl ether
(*b*) Ethyl methyl ether
(*c*) Dimethyl ether
(*d*) *n*-Propyl alcohol
Answer. (*b*)
433. Ethyl alcohol reacts with concentrated H_2SO_4 at 140°C to form
(*a*) Acetone
(*b*) Ethylene
(*c*) Diethyl ether
(*d*) Acetic acid
Answer. (*c*)
434. Ethers are kept in brown bottles because
(*a*) Brown bottles are cheaper than colorless clear bottles
(*b*) Ethers absorb moisture
(*c*) Ethers evaporate readily
(*d*) Ethers are oxidized to explosive peroxides
Answer. (*d*)
435. Ethers are stored in brown bottles. This is because on exposure to air and light ethers are converted to
(*a*) Peroxides
(*b*) Oxonium ions
(*c*) Ozonides

(*d*) Electrophiles
Answer. (*a*)
436. Ethers can be freed from peroxides by treatment with
(*a*) Ferrous salt
(*b*) Sodium carbonate
(*c*) Ferric salt
(*d*) Sodium bicarbonate
Answer. (*c*)
437. Which of the following statements is false?
(*a*) Diethyl ether has been used as a general anesthetic
(*b*) Ethyl alcohol is present in all alcoholic beverages
(*c*) Methyl alcohol is produced by fermentation of sugars
(*d*) Ethylene glycol is a common antifreeze for automobiles
Answer. (*c*)
438. Ethers react with cold concentrated H_2SO_4 to form
(*a*) Oxonium salts
(*b*) Alkenes
(*c*) Alkoxides
(*d*) Zwitterions
Answer. (*a*)
439. Which of the following reagents readily react with ethyl methyl ether?
(*a*) NaOH
(*b*) Conc HI
(*c*) $KMnO_4$
(*d*) H_2O
Answer. (*b*)
440. Diethyl ether reacts with sodium metal to give
(*a*) Ethanol
(*b*) Sodium ethoxide
(*c*) Ethanal
(*d*) Nothing happens
Answer. (*d*)
441. Diethyl ether on heating with excess concentrated HI gives
(*a*) Methyl iodide

(*b*) Isopropyl iodide
(*c*) Ethyl iodide
(*d*) *n*-Propyl iodide
Answer. (*c*)
442. Diethyl ether reacts with excess of hot concentrated HI to form
(*a*) CH_3CH_2I + CH_3CH_2OH
(*b*) Only CH_3CH_2OH
(*c*) CH_3CH_2OH + $CH_2{=}CH_2$
(*d*) Only CH_3CH_2I
Answer. (*d*)
443. Which is the best reagent to accomplish the following conversion?
$CH_3CH_2OCH_2CH_3 \xrightarrow{?} CH_3CH_2Br$
(*a*) Br_2 in CCl_4
(*b*) NaBr
(*c*) Br_2 in H_2O
(*d*) Conc HBr
Answer. (*d*)
444. Which of the following pairs of compounds will not form hydrogen bonds with each other?
(*a*) CH_3OH and CH_3CH_2OH
(*b*) CH_3SH and CH_3CH_2SH
(*c*) CH_3OCH_3 and $CH_3CH_2OCH_2CH_3$
(*d*) CH_3COOH and H_2O
Answer. (*c*)
445. The compound with the lowest boiling point is
(*a*) H_2O
(*b*) CH_3CH_2OH
(*c*) CH_3OCH_3
(*d*) $CH_3CH_2CH_3$
Answer. (*d*)
446. Which of the following would have the highest boiling point?
(*a*) 1-Butanol

(*b*) Butane
(*c*) 1-Butene
(*d*) 1-Butyne
Answer. (*a*). Alcohols of the same chain length as alkanes, alkenes, and alkynes have higher boiling points due to their ability to hydrogen bond.
447. Which of the following would have the highest boiling point?
(*a*) Dimethyl ether
(*b*) Diethyl ether
(*c*) Ethyl methyl ether
(*d*) Diisopropyl ether
Answer. (*d*). Ethers follow the same trend as alkanes, so diisopropyl ether will have the highest boiling point because it has the highest molecular weight.
448. Which of the following functional group series is ranked according to increasing boiling points?
(*a*) diethyl ether, ethane, ethanol, ethanethiol
(*b*) ethane, ethanol, diethyl ether, ethanethiol
(*c*) ethane, diethyl ether, ethanethiol, ethanol
(*d*) diethyl ether, ethane, ethanethiol, ethanol
Answer. (*c*)
449. The following compounds have identical molecular weights. Which would have the lowest boiling point?
(*a*) 1-Methoxypropane
(*b*) 1-Butanol
(*c*) 1,1-Dimethylethanol
(*d*) 2-Butanol
Answer. (*a*)
450. Cyclic ethers with three-membered ring are called
(*a*) Lactones
(*b*) Oxiranes
(*c*) Alkoxides
(*d*) Epoxy resins
Answer. (*b*)

CHAPTER TWO

Objective Questions (451 to 1000)

451. Ethylene reacts with oxygen in the presence of silver catalyst at 300°C to form
(*a*) Diethyl ether
(*b*) Ethylene glycol
(*c*) Ethyl alcohol
(*d*) Ethylene oxide
Answer. (*d*)
452. Ethylene oxide reacts with HBr to give
(*a*) 1-Bromoethanol
(*b*) Ethyl bromide
(*c*) 2-Bromoethanol
(*c*) Ethylene glycol
Answer. (*c*)
453. Acid-catalyzed hydrolysis of ethylene oxide yields
(*a*) CH_3CH_2OH
(*b*) $HOCH_2CH_2OH$
(*c*) $CH_3CH_2CH_2OH$
(*d*) $HOCH_2CH_2CH_2OH$
Answer. (*b*)
454. The product of the reaction of ethylene oxide with acidic methanol is
(*a*) $CH_3OCH_2CH_2OH$
(*b*) $CH_3CH_2CH_2CH_2OH$
(*c*) $HOCH_2CH_2OH$
(*d*) $CH_3CH_2OCH_2CH_3$
Answer. (*a*)
455. Ethylene oxide reacts with ammonia to give
(*a*) 1-Aminoethanol
(*b*) Ethylamine
(*c*) 2-Aminoethanol
(*d*) Acetamide
Answer. (*c*)
456. Which of the following is closest to the C–O–C bond angle in CH_3–O–CH_3?
(*a*) 180°
(*b*) 120°

(*c*) 109.5°
(*d*) 90°
Answer. (*c*)
457. When dipentyl ether is treated with excess HI, through what type of mechanism(s) does the major product result?
(*a*) S_N2
(*b*) S_N1
(*c*) E1
(*d*) E2
Answer. (*a*)
458. Which of the following is *not* a property of thiols (RSH)?
(*a*) They are all solids
(*b*) They can be oxidized to disulfides
(*c*) They have foul odors
(*d*) They are weak acids
Answer. (*a*)
459. Thiols are alcohol analogs in which the oxygen has been replaced by sulfur (e.g., CH_3SH). Given the fact that the S–H bond is less polar than the O–H bond, which of the following statements comparing thiols and alcohols is correct?
(*a*) Hydrogen bonding forces are weaker in thiols.
(*b*) Hydrogen bonding forces are stronger in thiols.
(*c*) Hydrogen bonding forces would be the same.
(*d*) No comparison can be made without additional information.
Answer. (*a*)
460. Which of the following has the lowest boiling point?
(*a*) CH_3CH_2OH
(*b*) $CH_3CH_2CH_2SH$
(*c*) $HOCH_2CH_2OH$
(*d*) $CH_3CH_2CH_2OH$
Answer. (*b*)
461. Which of the following is least soluble in water?
(*a*) CH_3OH

(*b*) CH_3CH_2OH
(*c*) CH_3SH
(*d*) $HOCH_2CH_2OH$
Answer. (*c*)
462. *n*-Butyl bromide reacts with NaSH to give
(*a*) $CH_3CH_2CH_2SH$
(*b*) CH_3SCH_3
(*c*) $CH_3CH_2CH_2CH_2SH$
(*d*) $CH_3CH_2SCH_2CH_3$
Answer. (*c*)
463. The carbon atom of a carbonyl group is
(*a*) *sp* hybridized
(*b*) sp^2 hybridized
(*c*) sp^3 hybridized
(*d*) None of these
Answer. (*b*). Whenever carbon is bonded to three other atoms or groups, it uses *sp*2 hybrid orbitals to form its bonds.
464. Which statement about the carbonyl group is NOT true?
(*a*) The carbonyl carbon is sp^2 hybridized.
(*b*) The bond angles among the three atoms attached to the carbonyl carbon are 120°.
(*c*) The three atoms attached to the carbonyl carbon form a nonplanar geometry.
(*d*) The carbonyl group forms resonance structures.
Answer. (*c*)
465. Acetone contains
(*a*) nine σ bonds plus one π bond
(*b*) ten σ bonds
(*c*) eight σ bonds plus two π bonds
(*d*) nine π bonds plus one σ bond
Answer. (*a*)
466. Formalin is
(*a*) 10% solution of formaldehyde in water
(*b*) 20% solution of formaldehyde in water

(*c*) 40% solution of formaldehyde in water
(*d*) 80% solution of formaldehyde in water
Answer. (*c*)
467. Which of the following will have the highest boiling point?
(*a*) Propanone
(*b*) 2-Pentanone
(*c*) Butanone
(*d*) 2-Hexanone
Answer. (*d*). Boiling points increase with molecular weight. The higher the molecular weight, the higher is the boiling point. All of the given compounds are ketones. 2-Hexanone has the highest molecular weight.
468. Which of the following will have the highest boiling point?
(*a*) Methanal
(*b*) Ethanal
(*c*) Propanal
(*d*) Butanal
Answer. (*d*). The boiling points increase with molecular weight. All of the given compounds are aldehydes. Butanal has the highest molecular weight.
469. What property of low-molecular weight aldehydes and ketones accounts for the magnitude of their boiling points?
(*a*) The ability to form strong H-bonds between their molecules.
(*b*) The ability of the carbonyl oxygen to form H-bonds with other carbonyl groups.
(*c*) The ability of the polar carbonyl group to attract other polar molecules.
(*d*) The ability of the carbonyl group to attract electrophiles and form bonds.
Answer. (*c*)
470. Primary alcohols have boiling points that are ____________ the corresponding aldehydes.
(*a*) Lower than

(*b*) Higher than
(*c*) About the same
Answer. (*b*). For compounds of similar molecular weights, boiling points increase with the degree of hydrogen bonding. *Remember* : Alcohols form strong hydrogen bonds and will boil at a higher temperature than the corresponding aldehydes.
471. The melting points of aldehydes and ketones tend to :
(*a*) decrease with increasing molecular weight.
(*b*) increase with increasing molecular weight.
(*c*) remain unchanged with increasing molecular weight.
(*d*) be unpredictable due to resonance.
Answer. (*b*)
472. Which action best accounts for the solubility of aldehydes and ketones in water?
(*a*) Polar interactions between solute molecules.
(*b*) H-bonding between solute molecules.
(*c*) Van der waals forces
(*d*) H-bonding between solute and solvent molecules
Answer. (*d*)
473. Ketones are prepared by the oxidation of
(*a*) Primary alcohol
(*b*) Secondary alcohol
(*c*) Tertiary alcohol
(*d*) None of these
Answer. (*b*)
474. Which of the following do you consider to be suitable for obtaining acetone (CH_3COCH_3)?
(*a*) Heating $CH_3CH_2CH_2OH$ with acidic $Na_2Cr_2O_7$
(*b*) Passing $CH_3\underset{}{\overset{OH}{\overset{|}{C}}}HCH_3$ over heated copper
(*c*) Oxidation of $CH_3CH_2CH_3$ with concentrated HNO_3
(*d*) Heating $CH_3CH{=}CH_2$ with dilute H_2SO_4
Answer. (*b*)
475. Cyclopentanol undergoes oxidation to give :

(*a*) Cyclopentene
(*b*) Cyclopentanone
(*c*) Cyclopentane
(*d*) Cyclopentanal
Answer. (*b*)
476. Which statement about the carbonyl group of ketones and aldehydes is true?
I. It can attract nucleophiles.
II. It can attract electrophiles.
III. It tends to undergo addition reactions.
IV. It tends to undergo substitution reactions.
(*a*) I and III
(*b*) II and IV
(*c*) I, II, and III
(*d*) I, III, and IV
Answer. (*c*)
477. Which of the following compounds reacts with sodium bisulfite and ammoniacal silver nitrate solution?
(*a*) $CH_3CH_2-\overset{\overset{\displaystyle O}{\|}}{C}-OH$
(*b*) $CH_3CH_2-\overset{\overset{\displaystyle O}{\|}}{C}-H$
(*c*) $CH_3CH_2CH{=}CH_2$
(*d*) $CH_3C{\equiv}CCH_3$
Answer. (*b*)
478. Acetone reacts with HCN to form a cyanohydrin. It is an example of
(*a*) Electrophilic addition
(*b*) Electrophilic substitution
(*c*) Nucleophilic addition
(*d*) Nucleophilic substitution
Answer. (*c*)
479. Which of the following reagents will react readily with both aldehydes and ketones?
(*a*) Grignard reagent

(*b*) Fehling's reagent
(*c*) Tollens' reagent
(*d*) Schiff's reagent
Answer. (*a*)
480. Boiling acetaldehyde (CH_3CHO) reacts with chlorine gas to give
(*a*) $CH_3-\overset{\overset{\displaystyle O}{\|}}{C}-Cl$
(*b*) $CCl_3-\overset{\overset{\displaystyle O}{\|}}{C}-H$
(*c*) CH_3CHCl_2
(*d*) $CHCl_3$
Answer. (*b*)
481. The reaction of ethanal with one equivalent of methanol and a trace of an acid will give
(*a*) Acetal
(*b*) Hemiacetal
(*c*) Ketal
(*d*) Hemiketal
Answer. (*b*)
482. Acetone undergoes reduction with hydrazine in the presence of NaOH to form propane. This reaction is known as
(*a*) Clemmensen reduction
(*b*) Wolf-Kishner reduction
(*c*) Rosenmund reduction
(*d*) Reformatsky reaction
Answer. (*b*)
483. Acetone undergoes reduction with zinc amalgam in HCl to form propane. This reaction is known as
(*a*) Clemmensen reduction
(*b*) Wolf-Kishner reduction
(*c*) Rosenmund reduction
(*d*) Aldol condensation
Answer. (*a*)

484. Cannizzaro reaction is not given by
(*a*) Formaldehyde
(*b*) Trimethylacetaldehyde
(*c*) Acetaldehyde
(*d*) Benzaldehyde
Answer. (*c*)
485. When formaldehyde is treated with 50% NaOH solution, it undergoes
(*a*) Cannizzaro reaction
(*b*) Wurtz reaction
(*c*) Aldol condensation
(*d*) Hydrolysis
Answer. (*a*)
486. The reduction of a ketone
(*a*) always gives a primary alcohol
(*b*) always gives a secondary alcohol
(*c*) always gives a carboxylic acid
(*d*) always gives a ketal
Answer. (*b*)
487. Reduction of acetaldehyde with H_2/Ni gives
(*a*) Ethyl alcohol
(*b*) Acetic acid
(*c*) Ethylene
(*d*) Ethane
Answer. (*a*)
488. On reduction with $LiAlH_4$, which of the following compounds could yield an optically active compound?
(*a*) Propanal
(*b*) Propanone
(*c*) Butanal
(*d*) Butanone
Answer. (*d*)
489. The reduction of cyclohexanone with $LiAlH_4$ (or $NaBH_4$) will give
(*a*) an alcohol
(*b*) an organic acid

(*c*) an aldehyde
(*d*) a hemiketal
Answer. (*a*)
490. Aldehydes undergo oxidation with $KMnO_4/H^+$ to give
(*a*) Alcohols
(*b*) Acetals
(*c*) Ketones
(*d*) Acids
Answer. (*d*)
491. Oxidation of acetaldehyde with $Na_2Cr_2O_7/H^+$ gives
(*a*) Ethylene glycol
(*b*) Acetic acid
(*c*) Ethanol
(*d*) Acetone
Answer. (*b*)
492. A hydrazone will result from the reaction of hydrazine with
(*a*) a phenol
(*b*) an aldehyde
(*c*) an alcohol
(*d*) an acid
Answer. (*b*)
493. Aldehydes can be distinguished from ketones by using
(*a*) Ammoniacal $AgNO_3$ solution
(*b*) Phenylhydrazine
(*c*) Saturated $NaHSO_3$ solution
(*d*) Thionyl chloride
Answer. (*a*)
494. The appearance of a silver mirror in Tollens' test indicates the presence of :
(*a*) an aldehyde
(*b*) a ketone
(*c*) an alcohol
(*d*) an alkene
Answer. (*a*)

495. Acetaldehyde on treatment with Tollens' reagent gives a precipitate of
(*a*) Ag
(*b*) $AgNO_3$
(*c*) Cu_2O
(*d*) None of these
Answer. (*a*)
496. Which of the following compounds will give a positive test with Fehling's solution?
(*a*) Formaldehyde
(*b*) Acetone
(*c*) Ethyl acetate
(*d*) Acetic acid
Answer. (*a*)
497. Acetaldehyde on treatment with Fehling's solution gives a precipitate of
(*a*) Cu
(*b*) Cu_2O
(*c*) CuO
(*d*) None of these
Answer. (*b*)
498. Which of the following will react with Fehling's solution giving a red precipitate?
(*a*) CH_3CH_2CHO
(*b*) $CH_3CH_2OCH_2CH_3$
(*c*) $CH_3CH_2CH_2OH$
(*d*) $CH_3-\overset{\overset{\displaystyle O}{\|}}{C}-CH_3$
Answer. (*a*)
499. Which of the following compounds will give an iodoform test?
(*a*) Benzoic acid
(*b*) Ethanol
(*c*) Benzyl chloride
(*d*) Methanol

Answer. (*b*)

500. Which of the following compounds does not give a positive iodoform test :

(*a*) Ethanol
(*b*) Ethanal
(*c*) Methanol
(*d*) Propanone

Answer. (*c*)

501. Which of the following compounds does not give iodoform test on treatment with
I_2/NaOH?

(*a*) Ethanol
(*b*) Propanone
(*c*) 2-Propanol
(*d*) Butanone

Answer. (*d*)

502. Which of the following compounds will give a positive iodoform test?

(*a*) Benzaldehyde
(*b*) 2-Pentanone
(*c*) 3-Hexanone
(*d*) 3-Pentanone

Answer. (*b*)

503. An organic compound (A), C_3H_8O, on oxidation gives (B), C_3H_6O. The compound (A) could be

(*a*) an aldehyde
(*b*) a ketone
(*c*) an alcohol
(*d*) an ester

Answer. (*c*)

504. An organic compound (A), C_3H_8O, on oxidation gives (B), C_3H_6O. The compound (B) could be

(*a*) a carbonyl compound
(*b*) an alcohol
(*c*) a carboxylic acid
(*d*) an ether

Answer. (*a*)

505. An unknown compound gave a positive Tollens' test. Treatment of the unknown with I_2/NaOH gave a solid which was identified as iodoform. The unknown was?

(*a*) Ethanal

(*b*) Acetone

(*c*) Propanal

(*d*) Acetophenone

Answer. (*a*)

506. A compound (A) gave a positive iodoform test, but did not reduce silver nitrate in ammonia solution. Compound (A) could be

(*a*) $CH_3-\overset{\overset{O}{\|}}{C}-H$

(*b*) $CH_3CH_2-\overset{\overset{O}{\|}}{C}-CH_2CH_3$

(*c*) $C_6H_5-\overset{\overset{O}{\|}}{C}-CH_2CH_3$

(*d*) $C_6H_5-\overset{\overset{O}{\|}}{C}-CH_3$

Answer. (*d*)

507. Which of the following characterizes the reactions of aldehydes and ketones?

(*a*) electrophilic addition

(*b*) electrophilic substitution

(*c*) nucleophilic acyl substitution

(*d*) nucleophilic addition; free radical addition

Answer. (*d*)

508. Why do aldehydes undergo nucleophilic addition reactions while esters undergo nucleophilic acyl substitution reactions?

(*a*) The carbonyl carbon of an ester is more electrophilic than that of an aldehyde.

(*b*) Aldehydes are more sterically hindered than esters.
(*c*) Once the nucleophile adds to an aldehyde, the tetrahedral intermediate is too sterically hindered to eliminate one of the attached groups.
(*d*) Once the nucleophile adds to an aldehyde, neither H− nor R− can be eliminated since they are strongly basic.
Answer. (*d*)
509. Which of the following reagents can be used to reduce acetaldehyde to ethyl alcohol?
(*a*) 1. $LiAlH_4$ / 2. H_3O^+
(*b*) 1. $NaBH_4$ / 2. H_3O^+
(*c*) H_2/Pt
(*d*) All of these
Answer. (*d*)
510. What is the hybridization of the carbonyl oxygen in carboxylic acids?
(*a*) *sp*
(*b*) sp^2
(*c*) sp^3
(*d*) s-sp^2
Answer. (*b*)
511. What is the hybridization and geometry of the carbonyl carbon in carboxylic acids and their derivatives?
(*a*) sp^3, tetrahedral
(*b*) sp^2, trigonal planar
(*c*) sp^2, tetrahedral
(*d*) sp^3, trigonal planar
Answer. (*b*)
512. Organic compound (A), C_4H_8O, does not react with sodium or PCl_5. However, it reduces an alkaline solution of a copper (II) salt on heating. Compound (A) could be
(*a*) an aldehyde
(*b*) a primary alcohol
(*c*) a ketone
(*d*) a secondary alcohol
Answer. (*a*)

513. Check the incorrect statement :
(*a*) Acetic acid is present in sour milk
(*b*) Formic acid is present in insect bites
(*c*) Tartaric acid is present in grapes
(*d*) Citric acid is a tricarboxylic acid
Answer. (*a*)
514. In the conversion of wine to vinegar
(*a*) Ethanol is oxidized to acetic acid
(*b*) Ethanol is reduced to acetic acid
(*c*) Methanol is oxidized to acetic acid
(*d*) Methanol is reduced to acetic acid
Answer. (*a*)
515. Vinegar is a
(*a*) 5% solution of acetic acid in water
(*b*) 25% solution of acetic acid in water
(*c*) 50% solution of acetic acid in water
(*d*) 40% solution of formic acid in water
Answer. (*a*)
516. In succinic acid, $HOOC(CH_2)_nCOOH$, *n* is equal to
(*a*) 1
(*b*) 2
(*c*) 3
(*d*) 4
Answer. (*b*)
517. In adipic acid, $HOOC(CH_2)_nCOOH$, *n* is equal to
(*a*) 1
(*b*) 2
(*c*) 3
(*d*) 4
Answer. (*d*)
518. The compound in which hydrogen bonding is not possible is
(*a*) CH_3OCH_3
(*b*) H_2O
(*c*) CH_3CH_2OH
(*d*) CH_3COOH

Answer. (*a*)
519. Which compound has the highest boiling point?
(*a*) CH_3CH_3
(*b*) CH_3OCH_3
(*c*) CH_3CH_2OH
(*d*) CH_3COOH
Answer. (*d*)
520. When carboxylic acids and dicarboxylic acids have similar molecular weights, how do their melting points compare?
(*a*) Carboxylic acids have greater melting points.
(*b*) Dicarboxylic acids have greater melting points.
(*c*) Both acids have similar melting points.
(*d*) No consistent trend exists.
Answer. (*b*)
521. The greater acidity of carboxylic acids compared to alcohols arises primarily from :
(*a*) the electron-donating effect of the hydroxyl group
(*b*) the electron-withdrawing effect of the carboxyl oxygen
(*c*) the acidity of α-hydrogens of carboxylic acids
(*d*) the resonance stability associated with the carboxylate ion
Answer. (*d*)
522. Which of the following statements is false about the acid-strength of acetic acid?
(*a*) Acetic acid is a stronger acid than monochloroacetic acid.
(*b*) Acetic acid is a stronger acid than propionic acid.
(*c*) Acetic acid is a weaker acid than trichloroacetic acid.
(*d*) Acetic acid is a weaker acid than formic acid.
Answer. (*a*)
523. Arrange the following compounds in order of decreasing acidity :

$BrCH_2CH_2COOH$ (1) $CH_3-CH(Br)-COOH$ (2) $CH_3-CH(F)-COOH$ (3)

(*a*) (1) > (2) > (3)
(*b*) (3) > (2) > (1)
(*c*) (3) > (1) > (2)
(*d*) (2) > (1) > (3)
Answer. (*b*)
524. Which of the following is the strongest acid?
(*a*) Formic acid
(*b*) Trichloroacetic acid
(*c*) Acetic acid
(*d*) Trifluoroacetic acid
Answer. (*d*)
525. Which of the following is the strongest acid?
(*a*) Butanoic acid
(*b*) 2-Chlorobutanoic acid
(*c*) 3-Chlorobutanoic acid
(*d*) 4-Chlorobutanoic acid
Answer. (*b*)
526. Which of the following is the strongest acid in aqueous solution?
(*a*) CH_3COOH
(*b*) $ClCH_2COOH$
(*c*) CH_3CH_2COOH
(*d*) $Cl_2CHCOOH$
Answer. (*d*)
527. Which is the strongest acid?
(*a*) CH_3COOH
(*b*) $Cl_2CHCOOH$
(*c*) $ClCH_2COOH$
(*d*) Cl_3CCOOH
Answer. (*d*)
528. Which of the following compounds is most acidic?
(*a*) CH_3COOH
(*b*) $ClCH_2COOH$
(*c*) CH_3CH_2COOH
(*d*) FCH_2COOH
Answer. (*d*)

529. Which of the following compounds is the strongest acid?
(*a*) CH_3COOH
(*b*) CH_3CH_2COOH
(*c*) CF_3COOH
(*d*) $CH_3CH_2CH_2COOH$
Answer. (*c*)
530. Which of the following compounds is least acidic?
(*a*) CH_3CH_2COOH
(*b*) $BrCH_2CH_2COOH$
(*c*) $CH_3-\underset{}{\overset{\overset{\displaystyle Br}{|}}{C}}H-COOH$
(*d*) $CH_3-\overset{\overset{\displaystyle F}{|}}{C}H-COOH$
Answer. (*a*)
531. Which of the following compounds is most acidic?
(*a*) CH_3CH_2COOH
(*b*) $BrCH_2CH_2COOH$
(*c*) $CH_3-\overset{\overset{\displaystyle Br}{|}}{C}H-COOH$
(*d*) $CH_3-\overset{\overset{\displaystyle F}{|}}{C}H-COOH$
Answer. (*d*)
532. Which of the following will give acetic acid on acid-hydrolysis?
(*a*) Ethyl acetate
(*b*) Acetone
(*c*) Methyl propionate
(*d*) Lactic acid
Answer. (*a*)
533. Propanenitrile undergoes acid-hydrolysis to give
(*a*) Formic acid
(*b*) Propionic acid
(*c*) Acetic acid

(*d*) Butyric acid
Answer. (*b*)
534. The characteristic reaction of carboxylic acids is :
(*a*) electrophilic addition
(*b*) electrophilic substitution
(*c*) nucleophilic addition
(*d*) nucleophilic substitution
Answer. (*d*)
535. Which of the following compounds will react with Tollens' reagent to give metallic silver?
(*a*) Formic acid
(*b*) Ethyl alcohol
(*c*) Acetic acid
(*d*) Acetone
Answer. (*a*)
536. Which of the following compounds on treatment with $NaHCO_3$ will liberate CO_2?
(*a*) Acetic acid
(b) Ethylamine
(*c*) Acetone
(d) Ethyl alcohol
Answer. (*a*)
537. Which of the following reagents will convert acetic acid into acetyl chloride?
(*a*) NaCl
(*b*) $HCl/ZnCl_2$
(*c*) $SOCl_2$
(*d*) HCl
Answer. (*c*)
538. Butyric acid reacts with PCl_5 to give
(*a*) Benzoyl chloride
(*b*) 1-Chlorobutane
(*c*) Butyryl chloride
(*d*) 1-Chloropropane
Answer. (*c*)
539. Acetic acid undergoes reduction with $LiAlH_4$ to give

(*a*) Ethanol
(*b*) Ethane
(*c*) Ethanal
(*d*) Ethyne
Answer. (*a*)
540. Acetic acid reacts with methyl alcohol in the presence of an acid catalyst to give
(*a*) Methyl formate
(*b*) Ethyl formate
(*c*) Methyl acetate
(*d*) Ethyl acetate
Answer. (*c*)
541. Calcium acetate on strong heating gives
(*a*) Methane + $CaCO_3$
(*b*) Ethane + $CaCO_3$
(*c*) Acetone + $CaCO_3$
(*d*) Ethane + CaO
Answer. (*c*)
542. $CH_3(CH_2)_4 CO\bar{O} \overset{+}{Na}$ is the sodium salt of hexanoic acid. The water solubility of this salt is :
(*a*) higher than that of hexanoic acid
(*b*) lower than that of hexanoic acid
(*c*) completely insoluble
(*d*) not predictable
Answer. (*a*)
543. Which of the following compounds has the lowest boiling point?
(*a*) 1-butanol
(*b*) butanoic acid
(*c*) butanenitrile
(*d*) methyl propanoate
Answer. (*c*)
544. Which of the following is the correct ranking in decreasing order of relative Boiling Point of carbonyl containing compounds?

(*a*) primary amide > carboxylic acid >> ester ~ acyl chloride ~ aldehyde ~ ketone
(*b*) ester > carboxylic acid >> amide ~ acyl chloride ~ aldehyde ~ ketone
(*c*) aldehyde ~ ketone > carboxylic acid >> ester ~ acyl chloride ~ amide
(*d*) carboxylic acid > amide >> ester ~ acyl chloride ~ aldehyde ~ ketone
Answer. (*a*)
545. Acetyl chloride undergoes nucleophilic substitution at a faster rate than methyl acetate because ________.
(*a*) the ester is more sterically hindered than the acid chloride
(*b*) the acid chloride is more sterically hindered than the ester
(*c*) the methoxide is a better leaving group than chloride
(*d*) chloride is a better leaving group than methoxide
Answer. (*d*)
546. Esters and amides are most easily made by nucleophilic acyl substitution reactions on :
(*a*) acid anhydrides
(*b*) carboxylates
(*c*) carboxylic acids
(*d*) acid chlorides
Answer. (*d*)
547. Which of the following conditions will drive the equilibrium of the Fischer esterification towards ester formation?
(*a*) addition of water
(*b*) removal of water as it is formed
(*c*) addition of alcohol
(*d*) both (*b*) and (*c*)
Answer. (*d*)
548. Which of the following statements describes the first step in the mechanism of the aldol condensation?

(*a*) An alpha hydrogen is abstracted by the base to form an enolate anion.
(*b*) A nucleophilic base attacks the carbonyl carbon atom.
(*c*) The carbonyl oxygen is protonated by the base ion.
(*d*) The alpha hydrogen is abstracted by an acid to the enolate anion.
Answer. (*a*)
549. Ammonium acetate on strong heating gives
(*a*) Urea
(*b*) Formamide
(*c*) Uric acid
(*d*) Acetamide
Answer. (*d*)
550. Which reaction does not yield an ester as one of the products?
(*a*) A carboxylic acid is heated with an alcohol
(*b*) A Grignard reagent is added to a carboxylic acid
(*c*) An acid halide is treated with an alcohol
(*d*) An alkyl halide is heated with the salt of a carboxylic acid
Answer. (*b*)
551. Silver acetate reacts with Br_2 to form methyl bromide, carbon dioxide, and AgBr. This is an example of
(*a*) Wurtz reaction
(*b*) Etard's reaction
(*c*) Hunsdiecker reaction
(*d*) Perkin reaction
Answer. (*c*)
552. Hunsdiecker reaction is used for the preparation of
(*a*) Alkyl chlorides and bromides
(*b*) Alkyl nitrates and nitrites
(*c*) Ketenes
(*d*) Alcohols
Answer. (*a*)
553. A compound undergoes reduction with $LiAlH_4$. It also dissolves in aqueous NaOH from which it can be recovered by addition of HCl. The compound is

(*a*) a carboxylic acid
(*b*) an ester
(*c*) an acid anhydride
(*d*) an alcohol
Answer. (*a*)
554. Acid chlorides undergo reduction to the corresponding aldehydes on treatment with hydrogen in the presence of Pd/$BaSO_4$. This reaction is called :
(*a*) Clemmensen reduction
(*b*) Rosenmund reduction
(*c*) Wolf-Kishner reduction
(*d*) None of these
Answer. (*b*)
555. Acetic anhydride is obtained by the reaction of :
(*a*) Acetic acid and sodium
(*b*) Acetic acid and water
(*c*) Acetic acid and diethyl ether
(*d*) Acetic acid and P_2O_5
Answer. (*d*)
556. Acetic anhydride reacts with ethanal to give
(*a*) Methyl acetate
(*b*) Methyl propanoate
(*c*) Ethyl acetate
(*d*) Ethyl propanoate
Answer. (*c*)
557. Acetamide on heating with P_2O_5 gives :
(*a*) Methylamine
(*b*) Ethylamine
(*c*) Methyl cyanide
(*d*) None of these
Answer. (*c*)
558. Acetamide is a much weaker base than ammonia. This is because
(*a*) the electron withdrawing effect of the C=O group makes the lone pair of electrons on nitrogen atom less available for protonation.

(*b*)) the electron withdrawing effect of the C=O group makes the lone pair of electrons on nitrogen atom more available for protonation.
(*c*) the presence of CH_3 group sterically hinders the protonation of the NH_2 group.
(*d*) an H atom from the nitrogen is less easily lost from CH_3CONH_2 than from NH_3.
Answer. (*a*)
559. Which of the following statements is *False* about acetamide?
(*a*) reacts with Br_2/NaOH to form tertiary amine
(*b*) undergoes acid-hydrolysis to form acetic acid
(*c*) undergoes dehydration with P_2O_5 to form a nitrile
(*d*) is a white crystalline solid, soluble in water
Answer. (*a*)

560. The C—C—O bond angle in $CH_3-\overset{\overset{\large O}{\|}}{C}-NH_2$ is approximately
(*a*) 60°
(*b*) 109.5°
(*c*) 90°
(*d*) 120°
Answer. (*d*)
561. Consider a small aliphatic 1° amine, 1° alcohol, ester, carboxylic acid, and amide, all of similar molecular weight. Which one is most likely to have the highest boiling point?
(*a*) The amide
(*b*) The alcohol
(*c*) The ester
(*d*) The carboxylic acid
Answer. (*a*). Amides can form very strong H-bonds because of ability of the *N* to donate electrons to the carbonyl (more so than OH of a carboxylic acid) and give the *O* considerable negative charge, thereby enhancing the H-bond acceptor capability of the molecule. Considering compounds of

similar molecular weight and carbon chain structure, the general trend is (highest to lowest boiling point) : amides, carboxylic acids, alcohols, amines, aldehydes/ketones/esters, alkynes, alkenes, and alkanes.

562. Which of the following acid-derivatives are most stable?
(*a*) Acid chlorides
(*b*) Esters
(*c*) Amides
(*d*) Anhydrides

Answer. (*c*). Amides are the most stable of the carboxylic acid derivatives because they have the most stable resonance forms :

$$R-\overset{\overset{O}{\|}}{C}-\ddot{N}H_2 \longleftrightarrow R-\overset{\overset{\bar{O}}{|}}{C}=\overset{+}{N}H_2$$

563. Which of the following will have the highest boiling point?
(*a*) Diethyl ether
(*b*) *n*-Butane
(*c*) Acetamide
(*d*) *n*-Propylamine

Answer. (*c*)

564. Acetamide can be converted into methylamine by
(*a*) P_2O_5
(*b*) Br_2/NaOH
(*c*) PCl_5
(*d*) $LiAlH_4$

Answer. (*b*)

565. Acetamide on reduction with $LiAlH_4$ gives
(*a*) Acetaldehyde
(*b*) Ethylamine
(*c*) Acetone
(*d*) Methylamine

Answer. (*b*)

566. Amides undergo hydrolysis under acidic conditions to give
(*a*) Carboxylic acid and amine
(*b*) Carboxylic acid and ammonium ion
(*c*) Carboxylate ion and ammonium ion
(*d*) Carboxylate ion and amine
Answer. (*b*)
567. By which of the following methods can CH_3CONH_2 be converted to CH_3CN?
(*a*) Oxidize with $Na_2Cr_2O_7/H^+$
(*b*) Heat with concentrated sulfuric acid
(*c*) Heat to 200°C
(*d*) Warm with P_2O_5
Answer. (*d*)
568. Which of the following reagents will react with acetamide to form methylamine?
(*a*) $LiAlH_4$
(*b*) $Br_2/NaOH$
(*c*) PCl_5
(*d*) H_2/Ni
Answer. (*b*)
569. Which of the following compounds does not form a salt with dilute HCl?
(*a*) $CH_3CH_2CONH_2$
(*b*) $(CH_3CH_2)_2NH$
(*c*) $CH_3CH_2NH_2$
(*d*) $(CH_3CH_2)_3N$
Answer. (*a*)
570. Propionamide on heating with a mixture of bromine and sodium hydroxide gives
(*a*) Propane
(*b*) Propylamine
(*c*) Propanol
(*d*) Ethylamine
Answer. (*d*)
571. What happens when urea is treated with hydrazine?

(*a*) Biuret is formed
(*b*) Semicarbazide is formed
(*c*) Carbon dioxide and nitrogen is formed
(*d*) Acetamide is formed
Answer. (*b*)
572. Carbonyl chloride reacts with ammonia to give
(*a*) Urea
(*b*) Acetone
(*c*) Acetamide
(*d*) Chloroform
Answer. (*a*)
573. Which of the following is not a constituent of normal urine?
(*a*) Albumin
(*b*) Urea
(*c*) Sodium chloride
(*d*) Uric acid
Answer. (*a*)
574. Esters can be formed by nucleophilic substitution reactions of :
(*a*) carboxylic acids and alcohols ; acid-catalyzed
(*b*) acid chlorides and alcohols
(*c*) both of the above
(*d*) neither of the above
Answer. (*c*)
575. The conversion $CH_3-\overset{\overset{O}{\|}}{C}-OCH_3 \longrightarrow CH_3CH_2OH$ is called :
(*a*) Oxidation
(*b*) Dehydration
(*c*) Reduction
(*d*) Hydrolysis
Answer. (*c*)
576. The following reaction is called :

$$CH_3CH_2-\overset{O}{\overset{||}{C}}-OCH_2CH_3 \xrightarrow[H_2O]{NaOH} CH_3CH_2-\overset{O}{\overset{||}{C}}-\overset{-}{O}\overset{+}{Na} + CH_2CH_2OH$$

(*a*) Saponification
(*b*) Condensation
(*c*) Elimination
(*d*) Esterification
Answer. (*a*)
577. Hydrolysis of an ester can be accomplished by :
(*a*) base-promoted hydrolysis
(*b*) acid-catalyzed hydrolysis
(*c*) both of the above
(*d*) neither of the above
Answer. (*c*)
578. Basic-hydrolysis of esters is called
(*a*) Acetylation
(*b*) Acidification
(*c*) Esterification
(*d*) Saponification
Answer. (*d*)
579. Base-catalyzed condensation of two ester molecules to form an alcohol and β-keto ester is called
(*a*) Claisen condensation
(*b*) Corey-House reaction
(*c*) Aldol condensation
(*d*) Transesterification
Answer. (*a*)
580. Ethyl acetoacetate undergoes *acid-hydrolysis* with dilute HCl to form
(*a*) Acetoacetic acid
(*b*) Succinic acid
(*c*) Acetic acid
(*d*) Adipic acid
Answer. (*a*)

581. The ethyl derivative of acetoacetic ester on basic-hydrolysis gives
(*a*) Acetic acid
(*b*) Acetic acid and propionic acid
(*c*) Propionic acid
(*d*) Acetic acid and *n*-butyric acid
Answer. (*a*)
582. Ethyl acetate on heating with sodium ethoxide gives
(*a*) Ethyl acetoacetate
(*b*) Sodium acetate
(*c*) Ethyl alcohol
(*d*) Diethyl ether
Answer. (*a*)
583. When ethyl acetoacetate is subjected to ketonic hydrolysis, the ketone obtained is
(*a*) Dimethyl ketone
(*b*) Methyl ethyl ketone
(*c*) Diethyl ketone
(*d*) Methyl *n*-propyl ketone
Answer. (*c*)
584. Ethyl acetoacetate reacts with phenylhydrazine to give
(*a*) Antipyrine
(*b*) Aspirin
(*c*) 4-Methyl uracil
(*d*) DDT
Answer. (*a*)
585. Keto-enol tautomerism is shown by
(*a*) Benzaldehyde
(*b*) Acetone
(*c*) Benzophenone
(*d*) Acetic acid
Answer. (*b*)
586. Fatty acids are
(*a*) Unsaturated dicarboxylic acids
(*b*) Long-chain alkanoic acids
(*c*) Aromatic carboxylic acids

(*d*) Aromatic dicarboxylic acids
Answer. (*b*)
587. Sodium or potassium salts of fatty acids are called
(*a*) Proteins
(*b*) Terpenes
(*c*) Carbohydrates
(*d*) Soaps
Answer. (*d*)
588. Soap is
(*a*) a mixture of salts of fatty acids
(*b*) a salt of glycerol
(*c*) a mixture of ethers
(*d*) a mixture of aromatic ethers
Answer. (*a*)
589. A wax is
(*a*) a nonpolar solid
(*b*) a long-chain alcohol
(*c*) a triacylglycerol
(*d*) none of these
Answer. (*a*)
590. Fats and oils are
(*a*) monoesters of glycerol
(*b*) diesters of glycerol
(*c*) triesters of glycerol
(*d*) diesters of glycol
Answer. (*c*). Fats are solid triesters of glycerol. Oils are liquid triesters of glycerol.
591. Fats differ from waxes in that fats have :
(*a*) More unsaturation
(*b*) Higher melting points
(*c*) A glycerol backbone
(*d*) Longer fatty acids
Answer. (*c*)
592. Oleic acid is a fatty acid containing
(*a*) 12 carbons
(*b*) 14 carbons

(*c*) 16 carbons
(*d*) 18 carbons
Answer. (*d*)
593. Both stearic acid and linoleic acid have 18 carbons. Linoleic acid is unsaturated, while stearic acid is saturated. The melting point of stearic acid :
(*a*) is higher than linoleic acid
(*b*) is lower than linoleic acid
(*c*) is same as linoleic acid
(*d*) can not predict, insufficient information
Answer. (*a*)
594. Liquid oils can be converted to solid fats by
(*a*) Hydrogenation
(*b*) Saponification
(*c*) Hydrolysis
(*d*) Oxidation of double bonds
Answer. (*a*)
595. Partial hydrogenation of vegetable oils in the presence of Ni catalyst at 200°C gives
(*a*) Vanaspati ghee
(*b*) Margarine
(*c*) Both of these
(*d*) None of these
Answer. (*a*)
596. Alkaline hydrolysis of oils (or fats) is called :
(*a*) Saponification
(*b*) Fermentation
(*c*) Diazotization
(*d*) Rancidification
Answer. (*a*)
597. Saponification of a fat
(*a*) always results in the formation of insoluble soaps
(*b*) produces glycerol and soap
(*c*) is used in the production of detergents
(*d*) is used in the production of lactic acid
Answer. (*b*)

598. Which of the following compounds will not be classified as lipids?
(*a*) Fats
(*b*) Waxes
(*c*) Soaps
(*d*) Oils
Answer. (*b*)
599. Synthetic detergents can be represented by the following general formula
(*a*) RONa
(*b*) $ROSO_3Na$
(*c*) RCOONa
(*d*) RCOOH
Answer. (*b*)
600. The degree of unsaturation of a fat can be determined by means of its
(*a*) Iodine number
(*b*) Octane number
(*c*) Saponification number
(*d*) Melting point
Answer. (*a*)
601. Which of the following statements is *not* true about fatty acids?
(*a*) Fatty acids are carboxylic acids with long hydrocarbon side chains.
(*b*) The double bonds in unsaturated fatty acids are always conjugated.
(*c*) Most naturally occurring fatty acids contain even numbers of carbons and are unbranched.
(*d*) Fatty acids can be saturated or unsaturated.
Answer. (*b*)
602. Which of the following best explains why the melting points of saturated fats increase with increasing molecular weight?
(*a*) decreased hydrogen bonding
(*b*) increased hydrogen bonding

(*c*) decreased intermolecular van der Waal's interactions
(*d*) increased intermolecular van der Waal's interactions
Answer. (*d*)
603. Which of the following terms best describes the compound below?

$CH_3(CH_2)_{12}CO_2H$

(*a*) a fatty acid
(*b*) an oil
(*c*) a wax
(*d*) a soap
Answer. (*a*)
604. Which of the following terms best describes the compound below?

$CH_3(CH_2)_7CH{=}CH(CH_2)_7CO_2H$

(*a*) an unsaturated fatty acid
(*b*) a triglyceride
(*c*) a synthetic detergent
(*d*) a micelle
Answer. (*a*)
605. Which of the following statements best describes the structure of waxes?
(*a*) long-chain unsaturated carboxylic acids
(*b*) long-chain saturated carboxylic acids
(*c*) long-chain esters
(*d*) short-chain esters
Answer. (*c*)
606. Which of the following terms best describes the compound below?

$CH_3(CH_2)_{26}CO_2CH_2(CH2)_{32}CH_3$

(*a*) a fat
(*b*) a wax
(*c*) a terpene
(*d*) an unsaturated triglyceride
Answer. (*b*)
607. Which of the following statements is *not* true about triacylglycerols?

(*a*) When solids and semisolids at room temperature, they are called fats.
(*b*) When liquids at room temperature, they are called oils.
(*c*) When hydrolyzed, they produce glycerol and carboxylate salts.
(*d*) Triacylglycerols with low melting points are composed of saturated fatty acids, causing them to be liquids at room temperature.
Answer. (*d*)
608. Triglycerides which are solids or semisolids at room temperature are called _________.
(*a*) oil
(*b*) fat
(*c*) steroid
(*d*) cholesterol
Answer. (*b*)
609. Which of the following statements is *not* true about phospholipids?
(*a*) They are similar to triacylglycerols except that the middle OH group of glycerol reacts with a phosphate rather than with a fatty acid.
(*b*) They constitute a major component of cell membranes.
(*c*) Phosphatidic acid is a phospholipid.
(*d*) The C-2 carbon of glycerol in phosphoacylglycerols has the R configuration.
Answer. (*a*)
610. The compound methylamine, $H_3C–NH_2$, contains a C–N bond. In this bond, which of the following best describes the charge on the nitrogen atom?
(*a*) slightly positive
(*b*) uncharged
(*c*) slightly negative
(*d*) –1
Answer. (*c*)
611. Triethylamine $[(CH_3CH_2)_3N]$ is a molecule in which the nitrogen atom is _________ hybridized and the CNC bond

angle is __________.
(*a*) sp^2; >109.5°
(*b*) sp^2; <109.5°
(*c*) sp^3; >109.5°
(*d*) sp^3; <109.5°
Answer. (*d*)
612. The N–H bond in the ammonium ion, NH_4^+, is formed by the overlap of what two orbitals?
(*a*) sp^3–sp^3
(*b*) sp^3–sp^2
(*c*) sp^2–sp^2
(*d*) sp^3–*s*
Answer. (*d*)
613. What is the hybridization of the nitrogen atom in CH_3NH_2?
(*a*) *sp*
(*b*) sp^2
(*c*) sp^3
(*d*) *s*-sp^3
Answer. (*c*)
614. What is the hybridization of the carbon atom in CH_3NH_2?
(*a*) 3sp^3
(*b*) *sp*
(*c*) sp^2
(*d*) sp^3
Answer. (*d*)
615. What type of intermolecular interactions does $(CH_3CH_2)_2NH$ undergo?
(*a*) induced dipole-induced dipole
(*b*) dipole-dipole
(*c*) hydrogen bonding
(*d*) all of these
Answer. (*d*)
616. Assuming roughly equivalent molecular weights, which of the following would have the highest boiling point?

(*a*) a tertiary amine
(*b*) a quaternary ammonium salt
(*c*) an alcohol
(*d*) an ether
Answer. (*b*)
617. Which of the following statements is *false* about primary amines?
(*a*) They can be prepared by reduction of nitriles with $LiAlH_4$.
(*b*) They do not form salts with acids.
(*c*) They react with ice-cold nitrous acid to form nitrogen gas.
(*d*) They are basic and soluble in water.
Answer. (*b*)
618. Which of the following statements is *false* about secondary amines?
(*a*) They react with chloroform and NaOH to form isocyanides.
(*b*) They can be prepared by reduction of isocyanides.
(*c*) They react with acid chlorides to give substituted amides.
(*d*) They react with ice-cold nitrous acid to give nitrosamine (yellow oil).
Answer. (*a*)
619. The hybridization of nitrogen in an amine is
(*a*) *sp*
(b) sp^3
(*c*) sp^2
(d) sp^4
Answer. (*b*)
620. Which of the following compounds is a secondary amine?
(*a*) $CH_3-\underset{}{\overset{NH_2}{\overset{|}{C}H}}-CH_3$
(*b*) $H_2NCH_2CH_2NH_2$
(*c*) $CH_3CH_2NHCH_3$

(*d*) $(CH_3)_3N$
Answer. (*c*)
621. A sample of pure amine molecules is found to possess no intermolecular H-bonding. This sample is most likely :
(*a*) 1° amine
(*b*) 2° amine
(*c*) 3° amine
(*d*) all of these
Answer. (*c*)
622. Which of the following is least soluble in water?
(*a*) Methylamine
(*b*) Trimethylamine
(*c*) Dimethylamine
(*d*) Aniline
Answer. (*d*)
623. Which of the following is most soluble in water?
(*a*) $CH_3CH_2CH_3$
(*b*) $CH_3-\overset{\overset{\Large I}{|}}{C}H-CH_3$
(*c*) $CH_3CH_2CH_2Cl$
(*d*) $CH_3CH_2CH_2NH_2$
Answer. (*d*)
624. Which amine is NOT soluble in water?
(*a*) Methylamine
(*b*) Dimethylamine
(*c*) Trimethylamine
(*d*) All are water-soluble
Answer. (*d*). Amines from H-bonds with water. Therefore, all low-molecular weight amines are soluble in water.
625. Consider a 1°, 2° and 3° amine, all of equivalent molecular weight. Which amine is most likely to have the lowest boiling point?
(*a*) 1° amine
(*b*) 2° amine
(*c*) 3° amine

(*d*) Not enough information to determine

Answer. (*c*). The 3° amines do not form hydrogen bonds to one another. The 1° and 2° amines can form hydrogen bonds to themselves and therefore have higher boiling points than 3° amines.

626. Which of the following will have the highest boiling point?

(*a*) Methylamine

(*b*) Diethylamine

(*c*) Ethylamine

(*d*) Triethylamine

Answer. (*d*)

627. Which compound has the highest boiling point?

1. $CH_3CH_2CH_3$ 2. CH_3CH_2OH 3. $CH_3CH_2NH_2$

(*a*) 1

(*b*) 2

(*c*) 3

(*d*) 2 and 3 have similar boiling points

Answer. (*b*). Amines are fairly polar, but they boil at temperatures lower than those of alcohols of similar chain length and structure. Amines do have higher boiling points than alkanes because they possess H-bond donors and acceptors.

628. Which of the following has the highest boiling point?

(*a*) $CH_3CH_2CH_2CH_3$

(*b*) $CH_3CH_2CH_2CH_2Cl$

(*c*) $CH_3CH_2CH_2CH_2NH_2$

(*d*) $CH_3CH_2CH_2CH_2F$

Answer. (*c*)

629. Amines are generally classified as

(*a*) Weak acids

(b) Strong acids

(*c*) Weak bases

(d) Strong bases

Answer. (*c*)

630. Acetamide reacts with Br_2/NaOH to give

(*a*) Methylamine
(*b*) Urea
(*c*) Ethylamine
(*d*) Acetyl bromide
Answer. (*a*)
631. Acetonitrile undergoes reduction with $LiAlH_4$ to form :
(*a*) Methylamine
(*b*) Dimethylamine
(*c*) Ethylamine
(*d*) Trimethylamine
Answer. (*c*)
632. Reduction of an imine will give an
(*a*) Acid
(*b*) Amide
(*c*) Amine
(*d*) Alcohol
Answer. (*c*)
633. Which of the following is most basic?
(*a*) Ammonia
(*b*) Methylamine
(*c*) Dimethylamine
(*d*) Trimethylamine
Answer. (*c*)
634. Alkyl halides react with ammonia in the presence of base to form :
(*a*) primary amines
(*b*) nitrated alkyl halides
(*c*) amides
(*d*) quaternary ammonium salts
Answer. (*a*)
635. The major product of the following reaction is :

$$CH_3CH_2Cl + (CH_3)_2NH \longrightarrow ?$$

(*a*) 1° amine
(*b*) 2° amine
(*c*) 3° amines
(*d*) amide

Answer. (*c*)
636. Aliphatic primary amines react with cold nitrous acid to form
(*a*) Alcohols
(*b*) Diazonium salts
(*c*) Nitriles
(*d*) Nitroalkanes
Answer. (*a*)
637. Which type of amine produces N_2 when treated with HONO?
(*a*) Primary
(*b*) Secondary
(*c*) Tertiary
(*d*) Quaternary
Answer. (*a*)
638. Methylamine reacts with nitrous acid to form
(*a*) CH_3CH_3
(*b*) CH_3OH
(*c*) CH_3NO_2
(*d*) CH_3CH_2OH
Answer. (*b*)
639. Which of the following compounds react with nitrous acid to form an alcohol?
(*a*) $CH_3CH_2NH_2$
(*b*) $(CH_3CH_2)_2NH$
(*c*) $(CH_3CH_2)_3N$
(*d*) 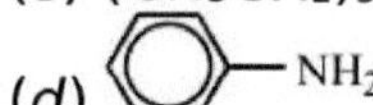

Answer. (*b*)
640. A nitrile can be made by dehydrating an amide. However, for this reaction to occur, the amide must be :
(*a*) primary
(*b*) secondary
(*c*) tertiary
(*d*) *N*-methylated
Answer. (*a*)

641. Which of the following amines react with nitrous acid to form nitrosoamine?
(*a*) Ethylamine
(*b*) Triethylamine
(*c*) Diethylamine
(*d*) Isopropylamine
Answer. (*c*)
642. Which of the following does not react with acyl chlorides to form amides :
(*a*) ammonia
(*b*) 1° amine
(*c*) 2° amine
(*d*) 3° amine
Answer. (*d*)
643. Hinsberg's reagent is
(*a*) Pd + $BaSO_4$
(*b*) *p*-Toluenesulfonic acid
(*c*) NH_2NH_2 + KOH
(*d*) Benzenesulfonic acid
Answer. (*d*)
644. Which of the following compounds will dissolve in aqueous NaOH after undergoing reaction with Hinsberg reagent?
(*a*) $CH_3CH_2NH_2$
(*b*) $(CH_3CH_2)_2NH$
(*c*) $(CH_3CH_2)_3N$
(*d*) $(CH_3)_3N$
Answer. (*a*)
645. Which of the following compounds does not react with acetyl chloride?
(*a*) Methylamine
(*b*) Dimethylamine
(*c*) Aniline
(*d*) Trimethylamine
Answer. (*d*)
646. A primary amine can be identified by using

(*a*) HCl
(*b*) $CHCl_3$
(*c*) NaOH
(*d*) $CHCl_3$ + KOH
Answer. (*d*)
647. Carbylamine test is given by
(*a*) Primary amines
(*b*) Secondary amines
(*c*) Tertiary amines
(*d*) None of these
Answer. (*a*)
648. Which of the following describes the side chain for Alanine?
(*a*) hydrogen
(*b*) ethyl group
(*c*) methyl group
(*d*) isopropyl group
Answer. (*c*)
649. Which of the following describes the side chain for Valine?
(*a*) ethyl group
(*b*) hydrogen
(*c*) isobutyl group
(*d*) isopropyl group
Answer. (*d*)
650. Which of the following describes the side chain of Leucine?
(*a*) ethyl group
(*b*) isopropyl group
(*c*) *sec*-butyl group
(*d*) isobutyl group
Answer. (*d*)
651. Which of the following amino acids has an aliphatic R group?
(*a*) Serine
(*b*) Cysteine

(*c*) Asparagine
(*d*) Leucine
Answer. (*d*)
652. Which of the following amino acids has an aromatic R group?
(*a*) Serine
(*b*) Cysteine
(*c*) Asparagine
(*d*) Tyrosine
Answer. (*d*)
653. Which of the following amino acids has a sulfur in the R group?
(*a*) Serine
(*b*) Cysteine
(*c*) Asparagine
(*d*) Tyrosine
Answer. (*d*)
654. Which of the following amino acids has a heterocyclic R group?
(*a*) Glycine
(*b*) Threonine
(*c*) Proline
(*d*) Aspartic acid
Answer. (*c*)
655. The α-carbon of all the amino acids is a chirality center except for __________.
(*a*) Glycine
(*b*) Threonine
(*c*) Proline
(*d*) Aspartic acid
Answer. (*a*)
656. Which of the following is correct for an amino acid solution when it is in the acidic form?
(*a*) $pH > pK_a$
(*b*) $pH < pK_a$
(*c*) zwitterionic

(*d*) pH = 7
Answer. (*b*)
657. When a disulfide linkage is formed, the compound containing this new linkage has been __________.
(*a*) hydrolyzed
(*b*) dehydrated
(*c*) electrolyzed
(*d*) oxidized
Answer. (*d*)
658. Which of the following structures can polypeptides have?
(*a*) primary structure
(*b*) secondary structure
(*c*) tertiary structure
(*d*) all of the these
Answer. (*d*)
659. Which of the following is the first step in the determination of the primary structure of proteins?
(*a*) determining the number and kind of amino acids in the peptide
(*b*) reducing the disulfide bridges in the protein
(*c*) protecting the *N*-terminal of the peptide
(*d*) protecting the *C*-terminal of the peptide
Answer. (*b*)
660. What are enzymes?
(*a*) saccharides that catalyze chemical reactions
(*b*) unsaturated fats that catalyze chemical reactions
(*c*) DNA molecules that catalyze chemical reactions
(*d*) proteins that catalyze chemical reactions
Answer. (*d*)
661. Which of the following may characterize the "secondary structure" of proteins?
(*a*) conformation of the protein backbone
(*b*) α-Helix
(*c*) parallel β-pleated sheet
(*d*) all of the above

Answer. (*d*)
662. Which of the following is the "quaternary structure" of proteins concerned with?
(*a*) sequence of amino acids in the peptide chain
(*b*) description of the way the peptide chains are arranged with respect to each other
(*c*) location of the disulfide bridges in the peptide chain
(*d*) conformation of the protein backbone
Answer. (*b*)
663. Which of the following protein structures does "denaturation" destroy?
(*a*) primary and secondary structures
(*b*) secondary and tertiary structures
(*c*) tertiary and quaternary structures
(*d*) secondary, tertiary, and quaternary structures
Answer. (*d*)
664. Which of the following are capable of denaturing proteins?
(*a*) organic solvents
(*b*) extreme pH
(*c*) heat
(*d*) all of the these
Answer. (*d*)
665. The monomeric units that make up peptides and protein polymers are __________.
(*a*) nucleic acids
(*b*) amino acids
(*c*) oligosaccharides
(*d*) amylopectins
Answer. (*b*)
666. A zwitterion is
(*a*) an ion that is positively charged in solution
(*b*) an ion that is negatively charged in solution
(*c*) a compound that can ionize both as a base and an acid.
(*d*) a carbohydrate with an electrical charge.
Answer. (*c*)

667. A zwitterion has which of the following properties
(*a*) no net charge
(*b*) a high melting point
(*c*) soluble in water
(*d*) all of these
Answer. (*d*)
668. An aqueous solution of glycine is neutral because of the formation of :
(*a*) Carbanion
(*b*) Zwitterion
(*c*) Carbonium ions
(*d*) Free radicals
Answer. (*b*)
669. Which one of the following compounds form zwitterions?
(*a*) carbonyl compounds
(*b*) amino acids
(*c*) phenols
(*d*) heterocyclic compounds
Answer. (*b*)
670. The pH at which the amino acid shows no tendency to migrate when placed in an electric field is known as its :
(*a*) Isoelectric point
(*b*) Dipole moment
(*c*) Iodine number
(*d*) Wavelength
Answer. (*a*)
671. The isoelectric point of a protein is
(*a*) the pH at which the protein molecule has no charges on its surface.
(*b*) the pH at which a protein in solution has an equal number of positive and negative charges.
(*c*) the electric charge under isothermal conditions.
(*b*) None of these.
Answer. (*b*)

672. Which of the following reactions is suitable for the preparation of α-amino acids?
(*a*) Schmidt reaction
(*b*) Hofmann's degradation of amides
(*c*) Strecker's synthesis
(*b*) Reduction of nitro compounds
Answer. (*c*)
673. Glycine is
(*a*) NH_2CH_2COOH
(*b*) $NH_2CH_2CH_2CH_2CH_2NH_2$
(*c*) $NO_2CH_2CH_2COOH$
(*b*) $BrCH_2COOH$
Answer. (*a*)
674. Glycine reacts with nitrous acid to form :
(*a*) Glycollic acid
(*b*) Diketopiperazine
(*c*) Methylamine
(*d*) Ethyl alcohol
Answer. (a)
675. When glycine is heated, it forms
(*a*) Diketopiperazine
(*b*) Acrylic acid
(*c*) Butyric acid
(*d*) Butyrlactam
Answer. (*a*)
676. Glycine is a unique amino acid because it
(*a*) has no chiral carbon
(*b*) has a sulfur containing *R* group
(*c*) cannot form a peptide bond
(*d*) is an essential amino acid
Answer. (*a*)
677. Which of the following organic ions results when glycine is treated with concentrated HCl?
(*a*) $\overset{+}{N}H_3CH_2COOH$
(*b*) $NH_2CH_2CO\bar{O}$

(*c*) $\overset{+}{N}H_3CH_2CO\bar{O}$
(*d*) $HOCH_2CO\bar{O}$
Answer. (*a*)
678. Proteins are
(*a*) polyamides
(*b*) Polymers of ethylene
(*c*) α-Aminocarboxylic acids
(*d*) Polymers of propylene
Answer. (*a*)
679. The five elements present in most naturally occurring proteins are :
(*a*) C, H, O, P, and S
(*b*) N, C, H, O, and I
(*c*) N, S, C, H, and O
(*d*) C, H, O, S, and I
Answer. (*c*)
680. The nitrogen content of proteins can be quantitatively determined by
(*a*) Carius method
(*b*) Kjeldahl's method
(*c*) Victor Meyer's method
(*d*) Rast method
Answer. (*b*)
681. Which of the following is the main structural feature of proteins?
(*a*) Peptide linkage
(*b*) Ester linkage
(*c*) Ether linkage
(*d*) α,β-Linkage
Answer. (*a*)
682. The linear arrangement of amino acid units in proteins is called :
(*a*) primary structure
(*b*) secondary structure
(*c*) tertiary structure

(*d*) quaternary structure
Answer. (*a*)
683. The primary structure of a protein refers to :
(*a*) whether the protein is fibrous or globular
(*b*) the amino acid sequence in the polypeptide chain
(*c*) the orientation of the amino acid side chains in space
(*d*) the presence or absence of an α-helix.
Answer. (*b*)
684. The α-Helix is a common form of
(*a*) Primary structure
(*b*) Tertiary structure
(*c*) Secondary structure
(*d*) None of these
Answer. (*c*)
685. The α-Helix is held in a coiled conformation partially because of :
(*a*) Optical activity
(*b*) Hydrogen bonding
(*c*) Resonance
(*d*) Delocalization
Answer. (*b*)
686. The double helical structure of DNA is held together by
(*a*) sulfur-sulfur linkages
(*b*) peptide bonding
(*c*) hydrogen bonding
(*d*) glycosidic bonds
Answer. (*c*)
687. Upon hydrolysis, proteins give
(*a*) Amino acids
(*b*) Hydroxy acids
(*c*) Fatty acids
(*d*) Alcohols
Answer. (*a*)
688. Complete hydrolysis of proteins produces :
(*a*) Ammonia and carbon dioxide
(*b*) Urea and uric acid

(*c*) A mixture of amino acids
(*d*) Glycogen and a fatty acid
Answer. (*c*)
689. Digestion of proteins involves
(*a*) changes in secondary structure only
(*b*) cleavage of peptide linkages
(*c*) removal of all carboxyl groups in the form of CO_2.
(*d*) removal of all NH_2 groups in the form of NH_3
Answer. (*b*)
690. Irreversible precipitation of proteins caused by heating is called :
(*a*) Polymerisation
(*b*) Denaturation
(*c*) Electrophoresis
(*d*) Inversion
Answer. (*b*)
691. Precipitation or coagulation of proteins may be caused by
(*a*) Heat
(*b*) Changes in pH
(*c*) Heavy metal salts
(*d*) All of these
Answer. (*d*)
692. Ninhydrin test is given by
(*a*) Carbohydrates
(*b*) Proteins
(*c*) Alkanes
(*d*) Alkenes
Answer. (*b*)
693. Which of the following tests is not used for testing proteins?
(*a*) Ninhydrin test
(*b*) Biuret test
(*c*) Xanthoproteic test
(*d*) Tollens' test
Answer. (*d*)

694. A protein solution on warming with concentrated HNO_3 may turn yellow. This test is called :
(*a*) Xanthoproteic test
(*b*) Ninhydrin test
(*c*) Biuret test
(*d*) Million's test
Answer. (*a*)
695. A compound gives a positive Tollens' test but negative Ninhydrin test. It is
(*a*) a protein
(*b*) an amino acid
(*c*) a monosaccharide
(*d*) pyridine
Answer. (*c*)
696. Cycloalkanes have the same molecular formula as :
(*a*) Alkanes
(*b*) Alkenes
(*c*) Alkynes
(*d*) Cycloalkenes
Answer. (*b*)
697. Which of the following compounds will give cyclopropane on treatment with sodium in dry ether?
(*a*) 1,3-Dibromopropane
(*b*) 1,1-Dibromopropane
(*c*) 1,2-Dibromopropane
(*d*) 2,2-Dibromopropane
Answer. (*a*)
698. Which of the following cycloalkanes is most reactive?
(*a*) Cyclopropane
(*b*) Cyclohexane
(*c*) Cyclobutane
(*d*) Cycloheptane
Answer. (*a*)
699. Which of the following compounds will react most readily with concentrated sulfuric acid?
(*a*) Ethane

(*b*) Cyclohexane
(*c*) Propane
(*d*) Cyclohexene
Answer. (*d*)
700. A compound of formula C_6H_{12} does not react with concentrated sulfuric acid. The compound could be
(*a*) Alkane
(*b*) Cycloalkane
(*c*) Alkene
(*d*) Cycloalkene
Answer. (*b*)
701. Which of the following molecules will decolorize bromine in carbon tetrachloride most readily?
(*a*) 1,2-Dimethylcyclopropane
(*b*) Cyclopentane
(*c*) 1,2-Dimethylcyclobutane
(*d*) Cyclohexane
Answer. (*a*)
702. Cyclopropane reacts with concentrated HBr to give.
(*a*) 1-Bromopropane
(*b*) Bromocyclopropane
(*c*) 2-Bromopropane
(*d*) 1,2-Dibromopropane
Answer. (*a*)
703. Cyclobutane reacts with hydrogen in the presence of nickel catalyst at 200°C to give
(*a*) Butane
(*b*) 1-Butene
(*c*) 2-Butene
(*d*) None of these
Answer. (*a*)
704. Cyclohexanol can be converted into cyclohexene by heating with
(*a*) Zn(Hg) and HCl
(*b*) Concentrated H_2SO_4
(*c*) $SOCl_2$

(*d*) H_2 and Ni
Answer. (*b*)
705. The bond angle between carbon atoms in cyclohexane is
(*a*) 109°28'
(*b*) 60°
(*c*) 90°
(*d*) 120°
Answer. (*a*)
706. Which of the cycloalkanes is not expected to have ring strain?
(*a*) Cyclopropane
(*b*) Cyclobutane
(*c*) Cycloheptane
(*d*) None of these
Answer. (*c*)
707. The bond angle between carbon atoms in cyclohexane is
(*a*) 60°
(*b*) 90°
(*c*) 109.5°
(*d*) 120°
Answer. (*c*)
708. Which of the following statements is false about cyclohexane?
(*a*) It is a saturated cyclic hydrocarbon
(*b*) All C–C–C bond angles are 109°28'
(*c*) It is very unstable, strained compound.
(*d*) It can exist in two conformations which are designated as the boat-form and the chair-form.
Answer. (*c*)
709. The most stable conformation of cyclohexane is the :
(*a*) Haworth form
(*b*) Boat form
(*c*) Newman form
(*d*) Chair form

Answer. (*d*)
710. What percentage of cyclohexane molecule is estimated to be in the boat form at any given time?
(*a*) over 99%
(*b*) between 90% and 99%
(*c*) approximately 50%
(*d*) less than 1%
Answer. (*d*)
711. Uriedes are
(*a*) Halogen derivatives of urea
(*b*) Acetyl derivatives of urea
(*c*) Alkyl derivatives of urea
(*d*) None of these
Answer. (*b*)
712. Uric acid on oxidation with alkaline $KMnO_4$ forms :
(*a*) Urea
(*b*) Barbituric acid
(*c*) Allantoin
(*d*) Caffeine
Answer. (*c*)
713. Diethyl malonate reacts with urea in the presence of sodium ethoxide to form
(*a*) Uric acid
(*b*) Barbituric acid
(*c*) Phenobarbital
(*d*) Barbital
Answer. (*b*)
714. A carbohydrate composed of three to ten sugar molecules is called a(n) :
(*a*) disaccharide
(*b*) oligosaccharide
(*c*) polysaccharide
(*d*) monosaccharide
Answer. (*b*)
715. All chiral D-sugars rotate plane-polarized light :
(*a*) clockwise

(*b*) counterclockwise
(*c*) +20.0°
(*d*) in a direction that cannot be predicted but must be determined experimentally
Answer. (*d*)
716. How many chirality centers are there in a 2-ketohexose?
(*a*) 2
(*b*) 3
(*c*) 4
(*d*) 5
Answer. (*b*)
717. How many stereoisomers are possible for a 2-ketohexose?
(*a*) 2
(*b*) 4
(*c*) 8
(*d*) 16
Answer. (*c*)
718. Which of the following statements best describes the difference between amylose and amylopectin?
(*a*) Amylose is a branched polysaccharide while amylopectin is a chain polysaccharide.
(*b*) Amylose is a straight-chain polysaccharide while amylopectin is a branched polysaccharide.
(*c*) Amylose contains α-1,6-glycosidic linkage which amylopectin does not contain.
(*d*) Amylose is composed of thousands of D-glucose units while amylopectin is composed of thousands of D-galactose units.
Answer. (*b*)
720. An aqueous solution of glucose behaves as an aldehyde because ________.
(*a*) it is hydrolyzed by water to the free aldehyde
(*b*) it is a ketone, but is in equilibrium with the aldehyde form

(*c*) glucose is actually a cyclic aldehyde
(*d*) its cyclic hemiacetal, the predominant form, is in equilibrium with the free aldehyde form
Answer. (*d*)
720. Which of the following statements best describes the meaning of "mutarotation"?
(*a*) a rapid exchange between the α and β forms of diastereomeric sugars
(*b*) a rapid exchange between the D and L forms
(*c*) a slow exchange between hydrogen and deuterated hydrogen
(*d*) a slow change in optical rotation to reach an equilibrium value
Answer. (*d*)
721. In solution, glucose exists as _________.
(*a*) the open-chain form only
(*b*) the cyclic hemiacetal form only
(*c*) the cyclic acetal form only
(*d*) an equilibrium mixture of the open-chain form and cyclic hemiacetal forms
Answer. (*d*)
722. Anomers of D-glucopyranose differ in their stereochemistry at _________.
(*a*) C1 (*b*) C2 (*c*) C3 (*d*) C4
Answer. (*a*)
723. Which of the following statements best describes the meaning of a "glycoside"?
(*a*) It is the mirror image of a sugar.
(*b*) It is the hemiacetal of a sugar.
(*c*) It is the acetal of a sugar.
(*d*) It is the enantiomer of a sugar.
Answer. (*c*)
724. Which of the following would give a positive Tollen's test?
(*a*) α-D-glucopyranose
(*b*) methyl β-D-glucopyranoside

(*c*) sucrose
(*d*) methyl α-D-ribofuranoside
Answer. (*a*)
725. Which of the following is true about sucrose?
(*a*) It hydrolyzes to fructose and glucose.
(*b*) It is a reducing sugar.
(*c*) It is a monosaccharide.
(*d*) It undergoes mutarotation in water.
Answer. (*a*)
726. Which term describes a sugar where one of the OH groups has been replaced with a hydrogen?
(*a*) amino sugar
(*b*) imino sugar
(*c*) dehydroxy sugar
(*d*) deoxy sugar
Answer. (*d*)
727. Monosaccharides are classified according to :
(*a*) the number of carbon atoms in the molecule.
(*b*) whether they contain an aldehyde or a ketone group.
(*c*) their configurational relationship to glyceraldehyde.
(*d*) all of the above.
Answer. (*d*)
728. Which is a monosaccharide?
(*a*) Sucrose
(*b*) Maltose
(*c*) Galactose
(*d*) Cellulose
Answer. (*c*)
729. Which is a disaccharide?
(*a*) Glucose
(*b*) Maltose
(*c*) Fructose
(*d*) Cellulose
Answer. (*b*)
730. Which of the following is not a monosaccharide?
(*a*) Ribose

(*b*) Fructose
(*c*) Sucrose
(*d*) Glucose
Answer. (*c*)
731. The designation D or L before the name of a monosaccharide
(*a*) indicates the direction of rotation of polarized light.
(*b*) indicates the length of the carbon chain in the carbohydrate.
(*c*) indicates the position of the OH group on the carbon next to the primary alcohol group.
(*d*) indicates the position of the asymmetric carbon atoms in the carbohydrate.
Answer. (*c*)
732. The principal sugar in blood is
(*a*) Fructose
(*b*) Glucose
(*c*) Sucrose
(*d*) Galactose
Answer. (*b*)
733. Glucose cannot be classified as
(*a*) a hexose
(*b*) an oligosaccharide
(*c*) an aldose
(*d*) a monosaccharide
Answer. (*b*)
734. Which of the following statements is false about glucose?
(*a*) it is a reducing sugar.
(*b*) it is a disaccharide.
(*c*) it has a pyranose form.
(*d*) it is a polyalcohol.
Answer. (*b*)
735. Which of the following statements is false about α-D-glucose?
(*a*) it has a pyranose ring.

(*b*) it is a hemiacetal.
(*c*) it shows mutarotation.
(*d*) it is the purest form of table sugar.
Answer. (*d*)
736. α-D-Glucose is different from β-D-glucose
(*a*) in the configuration at C-1
(*b*) because they are mirror images of each other
(*c*) because they are enantiomers
(*d*) because they are geometrical isomers
Answer. (*a*)
737. α-D-Glucopyranose is a(n) :
(*a*) hemiacetal
(*b*) hemiketal
(*c*) acetal
(*d*) ketal
Answer. (*a*)
738. The number of asymmetric carbon atoms in the α-D-glucopyranose molecule is :
(*a*) 2
(*b*) 3
(*c*) 4
(*d*) 5
Answer. (*d*)
739. Which of the following statements is false about an aldohexose?
(*a*) It is a monosaccharide.
(*b*) It contains a potential aldehyde group.
(*c*) α-D-Glucopyranose is an aldohexose.
(*d*) Fructose is an aldohexose.
Answer. (*d*)
740. All of the following monosaccharides give the same osazone except
(*a*) Galactose
(*b*) Glucose
(*c*) Fructose
(*d*) Mannose

Answer. (*a*)
741. Mutarotation is a term related to
(*a*) Interconversion of anomers
(*b*) Relationship of D- and L- families
(*c*) Hydrolysis of sucrose
(*d*) Number of monsaccharides in a carbohydrate
Answer. (*a*)
742. The mutarotation of glucose is characterized by :
(*a*) a change from an aldehyde to ketone structure.
(*b*) a change of specific rotation from a (+) to a (–) value.
(*c*) the presence of an intramolecular bridge structure.
(*d*) the irreversible change from α-D to the β-D form.
Answer. (*c*)
743. Which of the following statements is false about glyceraldehyde?
(*a*) Its IUPAC name is 1,2-dihydroxypropanal
(*b*) It is isomeric with 1,3-dihydroxypropanone
(*c*) It is optically active
(*d*) It shows mutarotation
Answer. (*d*)
744. Common table sugar is
(*a*) Glucose
(*b*) Sucrose
(*c*) Fructose
(*d*) Maltose
Answer. (*b*)
745. Which of the following carbohydrates is sweeter than sucrose?
(*a*) Glucose
(*b*) Fructose
(*c*) Lactose
(*d*) None of these
Answer. (*b*)
746. By approximately what factor is the sweetness of saccharin greater than that of sugar?
(*a*) 5

(*b*) 50
(*c*) 500
(*d*) 1000
Answer. (*c*)
747. Which of the following statements is false about sucrose?
(*a*) It is also called table sugar.
(*b*) It may be fermented by yeast to produce alcohol.
(*c*) It reduces Fehling's solution.
(*d*) It does not reduce Tollens' reagent.
Answer. (*c*)
748. The sugar that yields only glucose on hydrolysis is
(*a*) Lactose
(*b*) Sucrose
(*c*) Maltose
(*d*) Fructose
Answer. (*c*)
749. A reducing sugar will
(*a*) react with Fehling's test
(*b*) not react with Fehling's test
(*c*) have fewer calories
(*d*) always be a ketone
Answer. (*a*)
750. Which of the following carbohydrates is not a reducing sugar?
(*a*) Glucose
(*b*) Sucrose
(*c*) Fructose
(*d*) Lactose
Answer. (*b*)
751. Which of the following carbohydrates will not give a red precipitate of Cu_2O when heated with Benedict's solution?
(*a*) Maltose
(*b*) Glucose
(*c*) Sucrose

(*d*) Fructose
Answer. (*c*)
752. Which of the following compounds reduces Tollens' reagent?
(*a*) Glucose
(*b*) Sucrose
(*c*) Methanol
(*d*) Acetic acid
Answer. (*a*)
753. The reagent that can be used to differentiate an aldose and a ketose is :
(*a*) Bromine water
(*b*) Fehling's solution
(*c*) Tollens' reagent
(*d*) None of these
Answer. (*a*)
754. Starch
(*a*) is a trisaccharide.
(*b*) is also called amylose.
(*c*) is also called amylopectin.
(*d*) is a mixture of amylose + amylopectin.
Answer. (*d*)
755. The monosaccharide obtained by hydrolysis of starch is :
(*a*) D-Glucose
(*b*) Maltose
(*c*) D-Galactose
(*d*) D-Ribose
Answer. (*a*)
756. Which of the following statements is false about cellulose?
(*a*) It is a polymer of glucose molecules joined in β-1,4 linkages.
(*b*) It is a major component of cotton.
(*c*) It is used in the manufacture of Dacron fibres.
(*d*) It is used in the manufacture of Rayon fibres

Answer. (*c*)
757. Which of the following products is not derived from cellulose?
(*a*) Rayon
(*b*) Insulin
(*c*) Gun cotton
(*d*) Paper
Answer. (*b*)
758. Coal-tar is the main source of :
(*a*) Aromatic compounds
(*b*) Aliphatic compounds
(*c*) Heterocyclic compounds
(*d*) None of these
Answer. (*a*)
759. Which of the following fractions of coal-tar distillation contains benzene?
(*a*) Light oil
(*b*) Middle oil
(*c*) Heavy oil
(*d*) Anthracene oil
Answer. (*a*)
760. Which of the following fractions of coal-tar distillation contains naphthalene?
(*a*) Light oil
(*b*) Middle oil
(*c*) Heavy oil
(*d*) Anthracene oil
Answer. (*b*)
761. What is the term used for isomers that are in rapid equilibrium?
(*a*) keto-enol tautomers
(*b*) constitutional isomers
(*c*) conformational isomers
(*d*) *cis*-trans isomers
Answer. (*a*)
762. Aromatic hydrocarbons are also called :

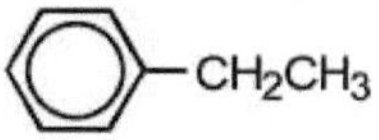

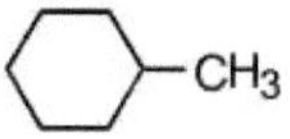

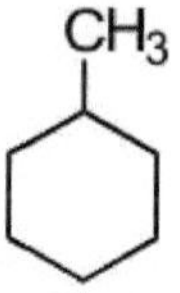

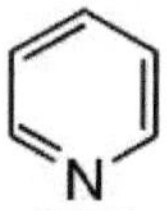

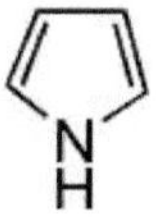

(*a*) Arenes
(*b*) Huckel's compounds
(*c*) Trienes
(*d*) Alkoxy compounds
Answer. (*a*)
763. Which of the following is an aromatic compound?
(*a*) $CH_3CH_2CH_2Br$
(*b*) $CH_3-\underset{}{\overset{CH_3}{\overset{|}{C}H}}-CH_3$
(*c*) $-CH_2CH_3$
(*d*) $-CH_3$
Answer. (*c*)
764. Which of the following compounds is *not* an aromatic compound?
(*a*) 
(*b*) CH_3
(*c*) N
(*d*) N H
Answer. (*b*)
765. Which of the following compounds is known as aniline?
(*a*) 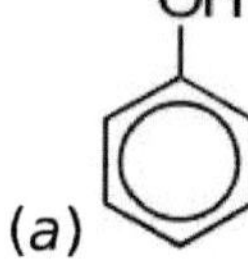

(*b*) CH_3–C_6H_5

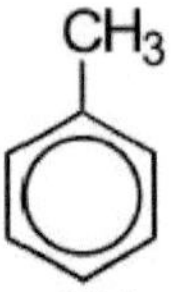

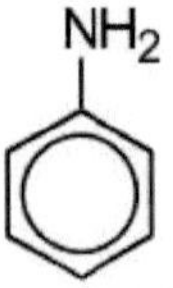

(*c*) NH_2–C_6H_5

(*d*) COOH–C_6H_5

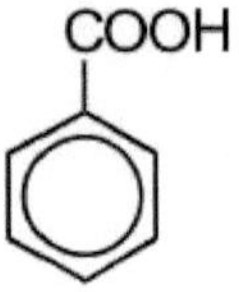

Answer. (*c*). (*a*) is Phenol, (*b*) is Toluene, and (*d*) is Benzoic acid.

766. Which of the following structures represent *m*-dichlorobenzene?

(*a*) Cl, Cl (cyclohexane ring, 1,3-positions)

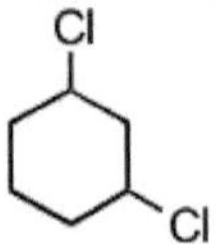

(*b*) Cl, Cl (benzene ring, 1,3-positions)

(*c*) Cl, Cl (benzene ring, 1,2-positions)

(*d*) Cl, Cl (benzene ring, 1,4-positions)

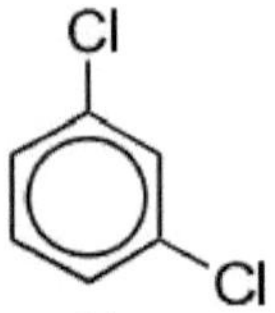

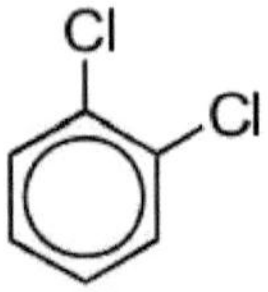

Answer. (*b*)
767. The best name for the following compound is :

Br, CH_3

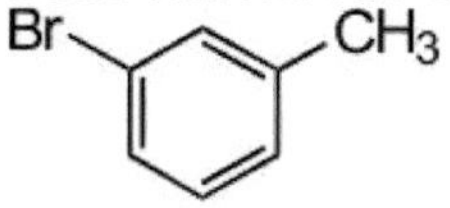

(*a*) 3-Methyl-bromobenene
(*b*) 3-Bromoaniline
(*c*) 3-Methylbromobenzene
(*d*) 3-Bromotoluene
Answer. (*d*)
768. The correct IUPAC name for the following compound is :

COOH, NO_2

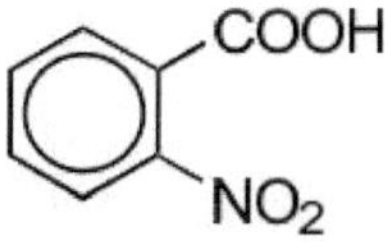

(*a*) *p*-Nitrobenzene methanoic acid
(*b*) *o*-Nitrobenzoic acid
(*c*) *o*-Nitrobenzene methanoic acid
(*d*) *m*-Nitrobenzoic acid
Answer. (*b*)
769. The correct IUPAC name for the following compound is :

F, OH, Cl

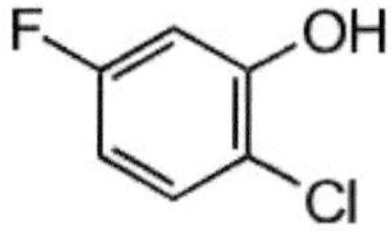

(*a*) 2-Chloro-5-fluoro-1-hydroxybenzene
(*b*) 1-Hydroxy-2-chloro-5-fluorobenzene
(*c*) 1-Fluoro-3-hydroxy-4-chlorobenzene
(*d*) None of these
Answer. (*d*). The name should be 2-Chloro-5-fluorophenol.
770. The correct IUPAC name for the following compound is :l

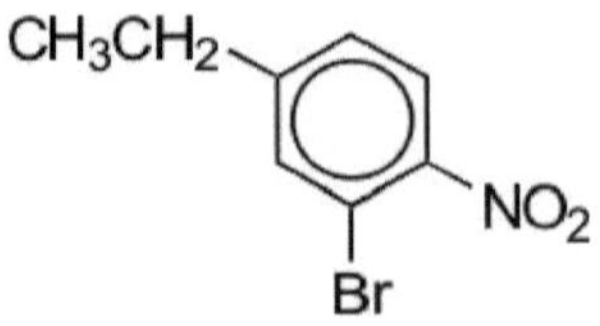

CH_3CH_2

NO_2

Br

(*a*) 3-Bromo-4-ethyl-1-nitrobenzene
(*b*) 1-Ethyl-2-bromo-4-nitrobenzene
(*c*) 2-Bromo-4-nitrotoluene
(*d*) 3-Bromo-1-ethyl-4-nitrobenzene

Answer. (*d*). The numbering is done to produce the smallest total. Therefore, number from the ethyl group toward the nitro group. List the substituents in alphabetic order.

771. Which of the following statements are correct concerning benzene?
(*a*) Benzene is a planar molecule.
(*b*) The six carbon-carbon bonds have the same length.
(*c*) Benzene has alternating single and double bonds.
(*d*) (*a*) and (*b*)

Answer. (*d*)

772. Which of the following statements is *incorrect* about benzene?
(*a*) All of the carbon atoms are *sp* hybridized.
(*b*) It has delocalized electrons.
(*c*) The carbon-carbon bond lengths are all the same.
(*d*) All twelve atoms lie in the same plane.

Answer. (*a*)

773. Which of the following statements about benzene is correct?
(*a*) All of the carbon atoms are sp^3 hybridized.
(*b*) It has no delocalized electrons.
(*c*) The carbon-carbon bond length is longer than that of ethane.
(*d*) It is a planar molecule.

Answer. (*d*)

774. The delocalized π system in benzene is formed by a cyclic overlap of 6 orbitals.

(*a*) *s*
(*b*) *p*
(*c*) *sp*
(*d*) sp^2
Answer. (*b*)
775. Aromatic molecules contain __________ π electrons.
(*a*) no
(*b*) 4*n* + 2 (with *n* being an integer)
(*c*) 4*n* + 2 (with *n* being 0.5)
(*d*) 4*n* (with *n* an integer)
Answer. (*b*)
776. Which of the structures below would be aromatic?

I II III IV

(*a*) I and IV
(*b*) I, III, and IV
(*c*) III and IV
(*d*) II
Answer. (*c*)
777. Which of the following is aromatic?
(*a*) cyclopentadienyl cation
(*b*) 1,3-cyclohexadiene
(*c*) cyclobutenyl anion
(*d*) cycloheptatrienyl cation
Answer. (*d*)
778. Which of the following is *not* a correct statement about the electrophilic substitution mechanism of benzene?
(*a*) Benzene functions as a nucleophile.
(*b*) Formation of a carbocation intermediate is the rate-determining step.
(*c*) The carbocation intermediate contains an sp^3 hybridized carbon in the ring.

(*d*) The addition product is a frequently observed minor product.

Answer. (*d*)

779. What purpose does $FeCl_3$ serve in the electrophilic aromatic substitution reaction between chlorine and benzene?

(*a*) It serves as a radical initiator to produce the chlorine radical needed to propagate the chain reaction.

(*b*) It functions by destabilizing the carbocationic intermediate and thereby increases the rate of H^+ loss.

(*c*) It serves as a Lewis base catalyst by reacting with Cl_2 to generate chloride ions.

(*d*) It serves as a Lewis acid catalyst by reacting with the Cl_2 and thereby activates it toward attack by benzene's π electrons.

Answer. (*d*)

780. Which of the following is *not* a correct statement concerning the Friedel-Crafts acylation of benzene?

(*a*) An alkyl group substitutes for a hydrogen.

(*b*) The benzene ring attacks an acylium ion.

(*c*) The acylium ion is resonance stabilized.

(*d*) The acylium ion is often produced from an acyl chloride.

Answer. (*a*)

781. What is the major organic product of the reaction between benzene and isobutyl chloride in the presence of $AlCl_3$?

(*a*) *tert*-butylbenzene

(*b*) isobutylbenzene

(*c*) *n*-butylbenzene

(*d*) chlorobenzene

Answer. (*a*)

782. Which of the following statements are *false* about benzene?

(*a*) It is a planar molecule with bond angles 120°.

(*b*) It is immiscible with water forming the lower layer.

(*c*) It can be converted into cyclohexane by hydrogenation at 200°C in the presence of Ni catalyst.

(*d*) It reacts with ethyl chloride in the presence of aluminium chloride to form ethylbenzene.

Answer. (*b*)

783. Which statement about the structure of benzene is *not* true?

(*a*) The two Kekule structures of benzene are in equilibrium.

(*b*) The carbon-carbon bond lengths in benzene are greater than the carbon-carbon double bonds in aliphatic compounds.

(*c*) The molecular geometry of benzene is best described as planar.

(*d*) The stability of benzene ring is much greater than the stability of 1,3,5-cycloheptatriene.

Answer. (*a*). Neither of the two Kekule structures for benzene has been isolated. No equilibrium exists between these two structures because they are resonance structures, differing only in the positions of electrons.

784. The carbon atoms in a benzene ring are :

(*a*) *sp* hybridized

(*b*) sp^3 hybridized

(*c*) sp^2 hybridized

(*d*) None of these

Answer. (*c*)

785. Which of the following compounds uses only $sp2$ hybridized carbons for bond formation?

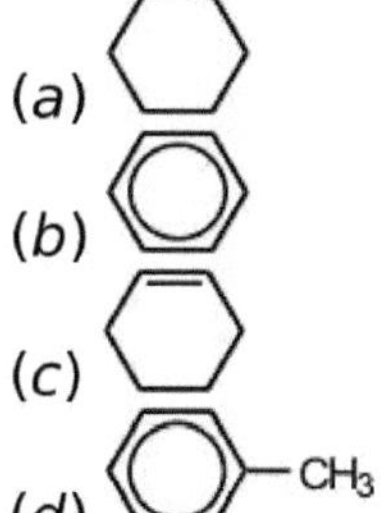

Answer. (*b*)

786. The C–C bond length in benzene is
(*a*) greater than the C–C bond length in ethane.
(*b*) shorter than the C–C bond length in ethylene.
(*c*) Same as that of C–C bond length in ethylene.
(*d*) intermediate between C–C bond length in ethane and C–C bond length in ethylene.

Answer. (*d*)

787. Which of the following compounds is aromatic?

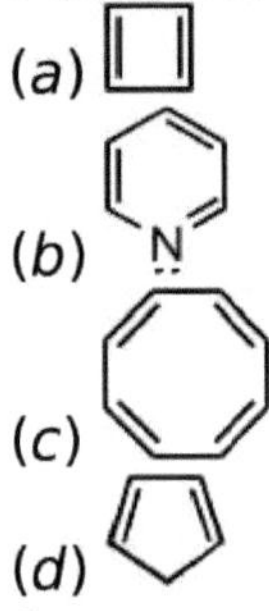

Answer. (*b*). Use the concept of aromaticity and Huckel rule to arrive at the correct answer.

788. Characteristic reactions of aromatic hydrocarbons are initiated by
(*a*) Electrophiles
(*b*) Nucleophiles
(*c*) Free radicals
(*d*) Uncharged molecules

Answer. (*a*)

789. Phenol on distillation with Zinc dust gives
(*a*) Phenylzinc
(*b*) Benzene
(*c*) Cyclohexanone
(*d*) Benzoic acid

Answer. (*b*)

790. Which of the following statements is *false* about toluene?

(*a*) can be prepared by treating benzene with methyl chloride in the presence of $AlCl_3$.
(*b*) is converted to benzoic acid on refluxing with acidic $KMnO_4$ solution.
(*c*) on refluxing with concentrated H_2SO_4 gives a mixture of *ortho* and *para* toluenesulfonic acid.
(*d*) can be nitrated with concentrated nitric acid to give a mixture of *ortho* and *meta* nitrotoluene.
Answer. (*d*)
791. Which of the following reagents will react with methyl group rather than the benzene ring in methylbenzene?
(*a*) Chlorine in the presence of uv light
(*b*) CH_3Cl in the presence of $AlCl_3$
(*c*) CH_3COCl in the presence of $AlCl_3$
(*d*) Hydrogen in the presence of nickel
Answer. (*a*)
792. Which of the following can be made by the action of CH_3Cl on benzene in the presence of aluminium chloride?
(*a*) Ethylbenzene
(*b*) *o*-Xylene
(*c*) Chlorobenzene
(*d*) *m*-Xylene
Answer. (*b*)
793. For reactions of ethylbenzene, the ethyl group is considered :
(*a*) *ortho* director
(*b*) *ortho-para* director
(*c*) *meta* director
(*d*) *ortho-meta* director
Answer. (*b*)
794. Toluene reacts with bromine in the presence of uv light to give
(*a*) *m*-Bromotoluene
(*b*) Benzyl bromide
(*c*) *o*-Bromotoluene
(*d*) Benzoyl bromide

Answer. (*b*)
795. Toluene reacts with chlorine in the presence of $AlCl_3$ to give
(*a*) *o*-Chlorotoluene
(*b*) *o*- plus *p*-Chlorotoluene
(*c*) *m*-Chlorotoluene
(*d*) *o*- plus *m*-Chlorotoluene
Answer. (*b*)
796. Toluene undergoes oxidation to give
(*a*) Benzyl alcohol
(*b*) Quinone
(*c*) Benzaldehyde
(*d*) Benzoic acid
Answer. (*d*)
797. Ethylbenzene undergoes oxidation with acidic potassium dichromate to give
(*a*) $C_6H_5-CH_2OH$
(*b*) $C_6H_5-C(=O)-H$
(*c*) $C_6H_5-C(=O)-CH_2CH_3$
(*d*) $C_6H_5-C(=O)-OH$
Answer. (*d*)
798. Oxidation of cumene with acidic $K_2Cr_2O_7$ gives
(*a*) Phenylacetic acid
(*b*) Benzaldehyde
(*c*) Benzyl alcohol
(*d*) Benzoic acid
Answer. (*d*)
799. Oxidation of toluene with chromyl chloride gives benzaldehyde. This reaction is known as
(*a*) Perkin reaction

(*b*) Benzoin condensation
(*c*) Etard's reaction
(*d*) Ozonolysis
Answer. (*c*)
800. Oxidation of *p*-xylene with acidic potassium dichromate gives
(*a*) HOOC–C_6H_4–COOH
(*b*) C_6H_5–COOH
(*c*) HOOC–C_6H_{10}–COOH
(*d*) H_3C–C_6H_4–COOH
Answer. (*a*)
801. Cresols on distillation with zinc dust gives
(*a*) *o*-Xylene
(*b*) Benzene
(*c*) *o*- plus *p*-Xylene
(d) Toluene
Answer. (*d*)
802. An organic compound (*A*) has a molecular weight 78 and an empirical formula CH. (*A*) is resistant to attack by oxidizing agents but undergoes substitution and addition reactions. X-ray analysis shows that the distance between adjacent carbon atoms is 1.39Å (intermediate between single and double bond lengths). The evidence suggests that compound (*A*) is
(*a*) Benzene
(*b*) Cyclohexane
(*c*) Toluene
(*d*) *n*-Hexane
Answer. (*a*)
803. Benzene undergoes substitution reaction more easily than addition reaction because

(*a*) it has a cyclic structure
(*b*) it has three double bonds
(*c*) it has six hydrogen atoms
(*d*) there is delocalization of electrons
Answer. (*d*)
804. Benzene reacts with concentrated HNO_3 in the presence of concentrated H_2SO_4 to give nitrobenzene. This reaction is an example of
(*a*) Electrophilic addition
(*b*) Nucleophilic addition
(*c*) Electrophilic substitution
(*d*) Nucleophilic substitution
Answer. (*c*)
805. Which of the following agents is used in order to make benzene react with concentrated nitric acid to give nitrobenzene?
(*a*) Concentrated H_2SO_4
(*b*) $FeCl_3$ catalyst
(*c*) Lindlar's catalyst
(*d*) Ultraviolet light
Answer. (*a*)
806. Which of the following agents is used in order to make benzene react with acetyl chloride to give acetophenone?
(*a*) Ultraviolet light
(*b*) $AlCl_3$ catalyst
(*c*) Platinum catalyst
(*d*) Al_2O_3 catalyst
Answer. (*b*)
807. Which of the following agents is used in order to make benzene react with bromine to give bromobenzene?
(*a*) Ultraviolet light
(*b*) Fe catalyst
(*c*) Nickel catalyst
(*d*) Al_2O_3 catalyst
Answer. (*b*)

808. In the Friedel-Craft acetylation of an aromatic ring, the role of the AlCl3 is to

(*a*) Form a $CH_3-\overset{\overset{O}{\|}}{\underset{+}{C}}$ ion.
(*b*) Function as a Lewis base
(*c*) Chlorinate the aromatic ring
(*d*) Withdraw electrons from the aromatic ring
Answer. (*a*)
809. The electrophile which is considered to be the active agent in the nitration of benzene is
(*a*) NO_2^-
(*b*) NO^+
(*c*) NO_2^+
(*d*) HNO_2^+
Answer. (*c*)
810. In chlorination of benzene, FeCl3 is used to generate
(*a*) Cl^-
(*b*) Cl^+
(*c*) Cl_2
(*d*) HCl
Answer. (*b*)
811. In sulfonation of benzene, the attacking species is
(*a*) H^+
(*b*) SO_2
(*c*) SO_3
(*d*) HSO_4^-
Answer. (*c*)
812. Consider the following reaction :

$$C_6H_6 + CH_3CH_2Cl \xrightarrow{(?)} C_6H_5CH_2CH_3 + HCl$$

The catalyst used to complete the above reaction is
(*a*) $LiAlH_4$
(*b*) $AlCl_3$

(*c*) Na
(*d*) KOH
Answer. (*b*)
813. Benzene reacts with H_2 at 150°C at 30 atm in the presence of Ni catalyst to give
(*a*) Cyclohexane
(*b*) Cyclohexene
(*c*) *n*-Hexane
(*d*) No reaction occurs
Answer. (*a*)
814. Benzene reacts with chlorine in the presence of $FeCl_3$ catalyst to form
(*a*) Hexachlorobenzene
(*b*) Chlorobenzene
(*c*) Hexachlorocyclohexane
(*d*) Benzyl chloride
Answer. (*b*)
815. Benzene reacts with acetic anhydride in the presence of $AlCl_3$ to form
(*a*) Acetophenone
(*b*) Benzophenone
(*c*) Phenylacetic acid
(*d*) Phenyl acetate
Answer. (*a*)
816. Benzene reacts with benzoyl chloride in the presence of anhydrous aluminium chloride to form
(*a*) Benzyl chloride
(*b*) Benzaldehyde
(*c*) Benzal chloride
(*d*) Benzophenone
Answer. (*d*)
817. Benzene undergoes Friedel-Crafts reaction with isopropyl alcohol in the presence of H_2SO_4 catalyst to give
(*a*) *n*-Propylbenzene
(*b*) Benzophenone
(*c*) Isopropylbenzene

(*d*) Nothing happens
Answer. (*c*)
818. Benzene reacts with propene in the presence of H_2SO_4 catalyst to give
(*a*) *n*-Propylbenzene
(*b*) Benzophenone
(*c*) Cumene
(*d*) Nothing happens
Answer. (*c*)
819. Ozonolysis of benzene gives
(*a*) Formic acid
(*b*) Glyoxal
(*c*) Formaldehyde
(*d*) Glycine
Answer. (*b*)
820. Gammexane is
(*a*) Hexachloroethane
(*b*) DDT
(*c*) Hexachlorocyclohexane
(*d*) TNT
Answer. (*c*)
821. Which group is an activating substituent?
(*a*) $-NO_3$
(*b*) –Cl
(*c*) –OH
(*d*) –F
Answer. (*c*)
822. Which of the following compounds reacts most rapidly with HNO_3/H_2SO_4?
(*a*) toluene
(*b*) anisole
(*c*) nitrobenzene
(*d*) benzonitrile
Answer. (*b*)
823. In electrophilic aromatic substitution reactions a chlorine substituent __________.

(*a*) is a deactivator and a *m*-director
(*b*) is a deactivator and an *o,p*-director
(*c*) is an activator and a *m*-director
(*d*) is an activator and an *o,p*-director
Answer. (*b*)
824. Which of the following substituents is an *ortho* and *para* director and ring deactivating?
(*a*) $-NH_2$
(*b*) $-Cl$
(*c*) $-OCH_3$
(*d*) $-OH$
Answer. (*b*)
825. Which of the following will undergo substitution in the *ortho* and *para* positions rather than in the *meta* position?
(*a*) Nitrobenzene
(*b*) Benzoic acid
(*c*) Acetanilide
(*d*) Benzaldehyde
Answer. (*c*)
826. Phenol is an *ortho-para* director because the hydroxyl group :
(*a*) donates electrons that increase electron density at *ortho* and *para* positions favoring nucleophilic attack.
(*b*) donates electrons that increase electron density at *ortho* and *para* positions favoring electrophilic attack.
(*c*) donates electrons to the *ortho* and *para* positions and attracts electrons away from *meta* positions favoring nucleophilic attack of the ring.
(*d*) donates electrons to the *ortho* and *para* positions and attracts electrons away from *meta* positions favoring electrophilic attack on the ring.
Answer. (*b*)
827. Compared to benzene, nitration of toluene takes place at
(*a*) Same rate
(*b*) Faster rate

(*c*) Slower rate
(*d*) Can not predict
Answer. (*b*)
828. Electron-withdrawing groups are *meta* directors because :
(*a*) the carbonium ion intermediate has a negative charge on the *meta* position.
(*b*) the more stable resonance hybrid occurs with *meta* attachment of the electrophile.
(*c*) the less stable resonance hybrid occurs with *meta* attachment of the electrophile.
(*d*) the carbonium ion intermediate has a positive charge on the *meta* position.
Answer. (*b*). When the electrophile attaches to the benzene ring, a carbonium ion is formed. This carbonium ion is relatively stable because the charge can be delocalized about the ring. *Ortho* or *para* attack results in a resonance form, with the positive charge on the carbon bearing the electron-withdrawing group (highly unstable). This resonance form does not occur with *meta* placement of the incoming electrophile.
829. Which compound undergoes substitution reactions faster than benzene?
NO_2
(*a*)
CH_3 C=O
(*b*)
Br
(*c*)

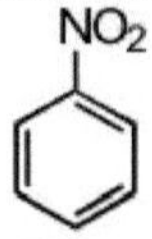

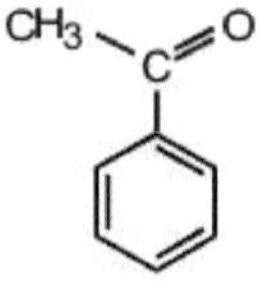

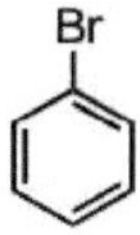

(*d*) NH_2 (benzene ring)

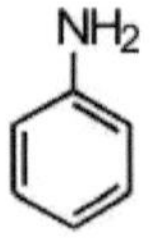

Answer. (*d*). Remember that activating (electron-donating) groups on benzene result in enhanced electrophilic substitution.

830. Which compound undergoes substitution reactions slower than benzene?

(*a*) OH (benzene ring)

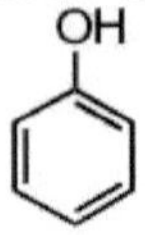

(*b*) $NHCH_3$ (benzene ring)

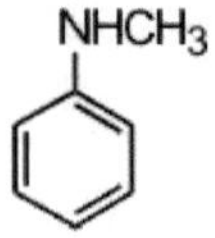

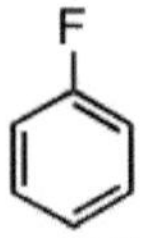

(*c*) F (benzene ring)

(*d*) OCH_3 (benzene ring)

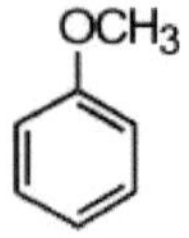

Answer. (*c*). The halogen (–F) is the only deactivating group because of its electronegativity and its low resonance potential.

831. Which of the following compounds undergoes nitration most readily?

(*a*) Benzene

(*b*) Toluene

(*c*) Nitrobenzene

(*d*) Benzoic acid

Answer. (*b*)

832. Which of the following compounds is most readily sulfonated?

(*a*) Benzene

(*b*) Chlorobenzene
(*c*) Toluene
(*d*) Nitrobenzene
Answer. (*c*)
833. *p*-Nitrotoluene on treatment with chlorine in the presence of $FeCl_3$ gives
(*a*) *m*-Chlorotoluene
(*b*) 2-Chloro-4-nitrotoluene
(*c*) *p*-Chlorotoluene
(*d*) 2-Nitro-4-chlorotoluene
Answer. (*b*)
834. How many isomeric dichlorobenzenes are there?
(*a*) 3
(*b*) 6
(*c*) 9
(*d*) 12
Answer. (*a*)
835. Which of the following compounds has maximum dipole moment?
(*a*) *p*-Dichlorobenzene
(*b*) *m*-Dichlorobenzene
(*c*) *o*-Dichlorobenzene
(*d*) Carbon tetrachloride
Answer. (*c*)
836. Which of the following reagents is most suitable for preparing chlorobenzene from benzene?
(*a*) Aqueous chlorine
(*b*) Chlorine in the presence of ultraviolet light
(*c*) Chlorine in acetic acid
(*d*) Chlorine in the presence of $FeCl_3$
Answer. (*d*)
837. Which of the reactions between the following pairs of reagents proceeds by a mechanism that may be described as an electrophilic substitution?
(*a*) Benzene + $Br_2/FeBr_3$
(*b*) Propene + Br_2

(*c*) Acetone + NH_2NH_2
(*d*) Ethyl bromide + *aq* KOH
Answer. (*a*)
838. Aryl halides are less reactive towards nucleophilic substitution as compared to alkyl halides due to
(*a*) Inductive effect
(*b*) Resonance stabilization
(*c*) Tautomerism
(*d*) Stereoisomerism
Answer. (*b*)
839. Which of the following compounds would be unaffected by boiling aqueous NaOH?
(*a*) Chloroethane
(*b*) Acetaldehyde
(*c*) Chlorobenzene
(*d*) Ethyl acetate
Answer. (*c*)
840. Hydrolysis of benzal chloride gives
(*a*) Phenol
(*b*) Benzaldehyde
(*c*) Benzyl alcohol
(*d*) Benzoyl chloride
Answer. (*b*)
841. Hydrolysis of benzotrichloride gives
(*a*) Benzophenone
(*b*) Benzoic acid
(*c*) Benzyl alcohol
(*d*) Phenol
Answer. (*b*)
842. Which reagent can be used to carry out the following conversion?

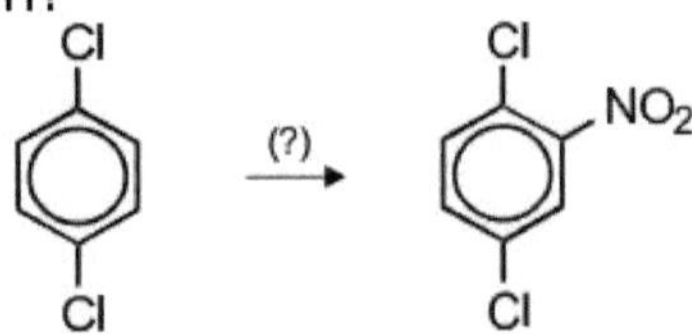

(*a*) $HNO_3 + H_2SO_4$
(*b*) $NaNO_2$
(*c*) $NaNO_2$ - HCl at 5°C
(*d*) NO_2
Answer. (*a*)
843. The following compound is called?

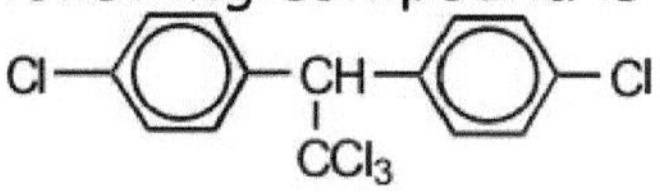

Cl–C₆H₄–CH(CCl₃)–C₆H₄–Cl

(*a*) Chloral
(*b*) DDT
(*c*) Lindane
(*d*) BHC
Answer. (*b*)
844. DDT is prepared by the reaction of chlorobenzene with (in the presence of conc. H_2SO_4)
(*a*) Chloral
(*b*) Chlorine
(*c*) Chloroform
(*d*) Carbon tetrachloride
Answer. (*a*)
845. Which of the following reagents can be used to distinguish between chlorobenzene and allyl chloride?
(*a*) H_2/Ni
(*b*) Br2 in CCl_4
(*c*) Zn/HCl
(*d*) NH_2NH_2
Answer. (*b*)
846. Which of the following reagents can be used to distinguish between chlorobenzene and benzyl chloride?
(*a*) alcoholic $AgNO_3$
(*b*) Br_2 in CCl_4
(*c*) KCN
(*d*) Br_2 in H_2O
Answer. (*a*)

847. An organic compound (*A*) was heated with a solution of NaOH. The resulting solution was cooled, acidified with dilute HNO_3, and then $AgNO_3$ solution was added. This gave a white precipitate. The compound (*A*) may be

(*a*) —Cl

(*b*) —CH_2Cl

(*c*) —COOH

(*d*) —CH_3

Answer. (*b*)

848. Which of the following statements is False/Incorrect about nitrobenzene?

(*a*) is formed by nitration of benzene at temperatures below 60°C.

(*b*) can be further nitrated to give *m*-dinitrobenzene.

(*c*) can be oxidized with $KMnO_4$ to give benzoic acid.

(*d*) can be reduced with Sn/HCl to give aniline.

Answer. (*c*)

849. Which of the following compounds reacts least rapidly in electrophilic substitution reactions?

(*a*) Nitrobenzene

(*b*) Phenol

(*c*) Bromobenzene

(*d*) Toluene

Answer. (*a*)

850. Nitrobenzene reacts with Br_2 in the presence of $FeCl_3$ to give

(*a*) *o*-chloronitrobenzene

(*b*) *o*-bromonitrobenzene

(*c*) *m*-chloronitrobenzene

(*d*) *m*-bromonitrobenzene

Answer. (*d*)

851. Nitration of nitrobenzene with HNO_3/H_2SO_4 gives :
(*a*) *m*-dinitrobenzene
(*b*) *o*-dinitrobenzene
(*c*) *p*-dinitrobenzene
(*d*) *m*-nitrobenzenesulfonic acid
Answer. (*a*)
852. Nitrobenzene undergoes reduction with zinc and KOH to give
(*a*) Aniline
(*b*) Hydrazobenzene
(*c*) Azobenzene
(*d*) None of these
Answer. (*b*)
853. Reduction of *p*-nitrotoluene with Sn + HCl gives :
(*a*) *p*-methylaniline
(*b*) Toluene
(*c*) *m*-methylaniline
(*d*) *N*-Methylaniline
Answer. (*a*)
854. Which of the following statements is false about aniline?
(*a*) It is a primary aromatic amine.
(*b*) It is a weak base which forms salts with acids.
(*c*) It liberates nitrogen on treatment with ice-cold nitrous acid.
(*d*) It can be prepared by the reduction of nitrobenzene with tin and HCl.
Answer. (*c*)
855. Which of the following statements is correct about aniline?
(*a*) is weak acid.
(*b*) diazotizes to benzenediazonium chloride when treated with ice-cold nitrous acid.
(*c*) can be nitrated with concentrated HNO_3 to form *p*-nitroaniline.

(*d*) gives an intense green color with a suspension of bleaching powder in water.
Answer. (*b*)
856. Which of the following statements is false about benzylamine?
(*a*) can be prepared by reduction of benzonitrile with $LiAlH_4$.
(*b*) cannot be prepared by reduction of benzamide with $LiAlH_4$.
(*c*) reacts with nitrous acid to give benzyl alcohol.
(*d*) reacts with $KMnO_4$ to give benzoic acid.
Answer. (*b*)
857. Aniline is prepared by
(*a*) the reaction of benzene with ammonia
(*b*) the reduction of nitrobenzene with Sn/HCl
(*c*) the dehydrogenation of nitrobenzene
(*d*) the reaction of nitrobenzene with I_2/NaOH
Answer. (*b*)
858. Benzamide reacts with Br_2 and KOH to give
(*a*) Benzene
(*b*) Benzylamine
(*c*) Aniline
(*d*) Benzonitrile
Answer. (*b*)
859. When ammonia is added to an alkyl halide, in the presence of base :
(*a*) primary amines form
(*b*) amides form
(*c*) nitrated alkyl halides form
(*d*) quaternary ammonium salts form
Answer. (*a*). Salts of 1° amines can be prepared from ammonia and alkyl halides. Treating the ammonium salt with base gives a 1° amine.

$$\ddot{N}H_3 + R{-}X \longrightarrow R{-}\overset{+}{N}H_3\,Cl^- \xrightarrow{NaOH} R{-}NH_2 + NaX + H_2O$$

860. Aniline reacts with bromine water to form
(*a*) Bromobenzene

(*b*) *m*-Bromoaniline
(*c*) 2,4,6-Tribromoaniline
(*d*) *o*- plus *p*-Bromoaniline
Answer. (*c*)
861. Which of the following will give a precipitate with excess bromine water?
(*a*) Bromobenzene
(*b*) Aniline
(*c*) Nitrobenzene
(*d*) Toluene
Answer. (*b*)
862. Aniline reacts with nitrous acid at low temperatures to give
(*a*) a *N*-nitrosoamine
(*b*) a nitrile
(c) a diazonium salt
(*d*) a nitrite salt
Answer. (*c*)
863. When aniline is heated with chloroform and alcoholic KOH, the product is
(*a*) Benzonitrile
(*b*) *p*-Chloroaniline
(*c*) Phenylisocyanide
(*d*) *m*-Chloroaniline
Answer. (*c*)
864. Aniline reacts with acetic anhydride to give :
(*a*) *N*-Methylaniline
(*b*) *p*-Aminoacetophenone
(*c*) Acetanilide
(*d*) *m*-Aminoacetophenone
Answer. (*c*)
865. Aniline undergoes oxidation with $Na_2Cr_2O_7/H_2SO_4$ to give
(*a*) Schiff's base
(*b*) *p*-Benzoquinone
(*c*) Phenol

(*d*) Benzoic acid

Answer. (*b*)

866. Which of the following reagents does not react with aniline?

(*a*) Acetyl chloride

(*b*) Acetic anhydride

(*c*) Ammonia

(*d*) Nitrous acid

Answer. (c)

867. Rank the following compounds in order of increasing base strength :

Cyclohexyl–NH_2 (1) C_6H_5–NH_2 (2) CH_3–C_6H_4–NH_2 (3)

(*a*) 1, 2, 3

(*b*) 3, 2, 1

(*c*) 2, 3, 1

(*d*) 2, 1, 3

Answer. (*c*). The aromatic amines are weaker bases than the nonaromatic cyclic amines because the lone-pair electrons on nitrogen are delocalized over the aromatic ring. This delocalization stabilizes the compound but also decreases the ability of the nitrogen to act as a base. Compound (3) is a stronger base than aniline because of the electron-releasing substituent on the ring.

868. Rank the following compounds in order of increasing base strength :

NH_3 (1) C_6H_5–CH_2NH_2 (2) C_6H_5–NH_2 (3)   Cl–C_6H_4–NH_2 (4)

(*a*) 1, 2, 3, 4

(*b*) 4, 2, 3, 1

(*c*) 1, 4, 3, 2

(*d*) 4, 3, 1, 2

Answer. (*d*). Of the aromatic amines, the weakest base is the one with the electron-withdrawing substituent: (4) is the weakest followed by aniline (3). Compound (2) is the strongest base because its electrons are not delocalized effectively into the aromatic ring, and it is therefore a primary amine, and its pK_a is slightly lower than that of ammonia.

869. Which of the following compounds is most basic?
(*a*) Aniline
(*b*) Benzylamine
(*c*) Acetanilide
(*d*) *p*-nitroaniline
Answer. (*b*)

870. Which of the following is most basic?
(*a*) CH_3NH_2
(*b*) $(CH_3)_3N$
(*c*) $(CH_3)_2NH$
(*d*) $-NH_2$
Answer. (*c*)

871. Which of the following is most basic?
(*a*) $(CH_3)_2NH$
(*b*) $-NH_2$
(*c*) $CH_3-\overset{O}{\overset{\|}{C}}-NH_2$
(*d*) NH_3
Answer. (*a*)

872. Which of the following compounds is most basic?

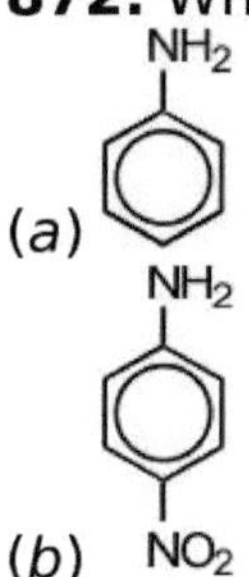

(*c*) m-Nitroaniline (NH_2, NO_2)

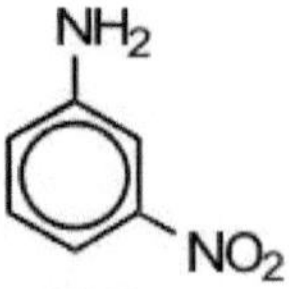

(*d*) C_6H_5–NH_2

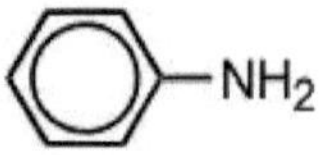

Answer. (*a*)

873. Which of the following is least basic?

(*a*) Aniline

(*b*) *p*-Nitroaniline

(*c*) Ammonia

(*d*) Trimethylamine

Answer. (*b*)

874. Which of the following is least basic?

(*a*) CH_3NH_2

(*b*) $(CH_3)_3N$

(*c*) $(CH_3)_2NH$

(*d*) C_6H_5–NH_2

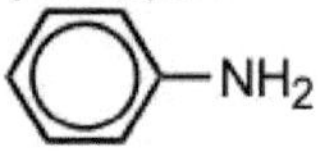

Answer. (*d*)

875. Which of the following compounds is least basic?

(*a*) Cyclohexylamine (NH_2)

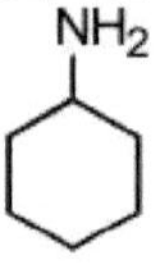

(*b*) Aniline (NH_2)

(*c*) o-Nitroaniline (NH_2, NO_2)

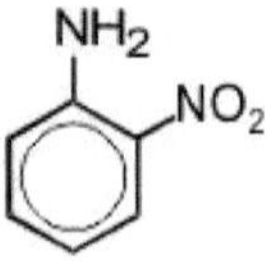

(*d*) 

Answer. (*c*)

876. Which of the following compounds will be most soluble in water at room temperature?

(*a*) Phenol
(*b*) Phenylammonium chloride
(*c*) Benzoic acid
(*d*) Benzylamine

Answer. (*b*)

877. The diazonium salts are the reaction products of the reaction of nitrous acid with

(*a*) primary aliphatic amines
(*b*) primary aromatic amines
(*c*) secondary aliphatic amines
(*d*) secondary aromatic amines

Answer. (*b*)

878. Preparation of a diazonium salt from a primary aromatic amine is known as :

(*a*) Coupling reaction
(*b*) Sandmeyer reaction
(*c*) Diazotization
(*d*) Corey-House synthesis

Answer. (*c*)

879. Which of the following reagents is used to prepare benzenediazonium chloride from aniline?

(*a*) $NaNO_2$ + HCl
(*b*) $LiAlH_4$
(*c*) NH_2NH_2 + KOH
(*d*) NaOH

Answer. (*a*)

880. Which of the following are optimum temperature conditions for making benzenediazonium chloride from

aniline?
(*a*) 0°C to 10°C
(*b*) 20°C to 25°C
(*c*) 30°C to 40°C
(*d*) 45°C to 50°C
Answer. (*a*)
881. Benzenediazonium chloride reacts with warm water to give
(*a*) Aniline
(*b*) Phenol
(*c*) Benzene
(*d*) Chlorobenzene
Answer. (*b*)
882. Bromobenzene can be prepared by treating aniline with
(*a*) Conc HBr
(*b*) $Br_2/FeBr_3$
(*b*) CuBr
(*d*) Nitrous acid *then* CuBr
Answer. (*d*)
883. Chlorobenzene can be prepared by treatment of aniline with
(*a*) Cuprous chloride
(*b*) Chlorine in the presence of UV light
(*c*) Nitrous acid followed by treatment with CuCl
(*d*) Chlorine in the presence of $FeCl_3$
Answer. (*c*)
884. Iodobenzene can be prepared by
(*a*) treating chlorobenzene with I_2 using $FeCl_3$ catalyst.
(*b*) treating phenol with I_2 in NaOH solution.
(*c*) treating benzenediazonium chloride with KI
(*d*) treating benzene with CH_3I using $AlCl_3$ catalyst.
Answer. (*c*)
885. Benzenediazonium chloride reacts with KI to form :
(*a*) Benzenediazonium iodide
(*b*) *m*-Diiodobenzene

(*c*) Iodobenzene
(*d*) *o*- plus *p*-Diiodobenzene
Answer. (*c*)
886. What is the major product of the following reaction?

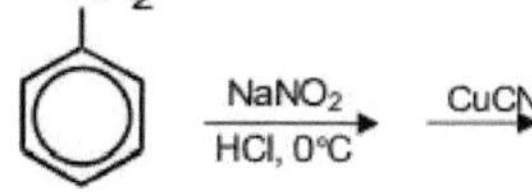

(*a*) Benzonitrile
(*b*) Benzoic acid
(*c*) Nitrobenzene
(*d*) Benzenediazonium chloride
Answer. (*a*)
887. Benzenediazonium chloride reacts with hypophosphorus acid to form :
(*a*) Phenol
(*b*) Benzaldehyde
(*c*) Aniline
(*d*) Benzene
Answer. (*d*)
888. Benzenediazonium chloride reacts with phenol to form :
(*a*) *p*-chlorophenol
(*b*) Chlorobenzene
(*c*) *p*-Hydroxyazobenzene
(*d*) DDT
Answer. (*c*)
889. Phenol is used
(*a*) in alcoholic beverages
(*b*) as anesthetic
(*c*) in antiseptics
(*d*) as moth repellant
Answer. (*c*)
890. Which of the following compounds is aspirin
(*a*) Methyl salicylate
(*b*) Salicylic acid

(*c*) Phenyl salicylate
(*d*) Acetylsalicylic acid
Answer. (*d*)
891. When phenol is treated with neutral $FeCl_3$ solution, it develops
(*a*) Violet color
(*b*) Yellow color
(*c*) Green color
(*d*) Nothing happens
Answer. (*a*)
892. Which of the following compounds will react with PCl_5 least vigorously?
(*a*) Ethanol
(*b*) Acetic acid
(*c*) Phenol
(*d*) Benzoic acid
Answer. (*c*)
893. Sodium phenoxide reacts with CO_2 at 125°C under 5 atm pressure to give salicylic acid. This reaction is called
(*a*) Kolbe's reaction
(*b*) Perkin reaction
(*c*) Wurtz reaction
(*d*) HVZ reaction
Answer. (*a*)
894. Phenol reacts with excess bromine water to give
(*a*) *o*- plus *p*-Bromophenol
(*b*) Bromobenzene
(*c*) 2,4,6-Tribromophenol
(*d*) *m*-Bromophenol
Answer. (*c*)
895. Resorcinol on distillation with zinc dust gives
(*a*) Benzene
(*b*) Cyclohexane
(*c*) Toluene
(*d*) *m*-Xylene
Answer. (*a*)

896. Bakelite has the following characteristics
(*a*) A polymer made from phenol and formaldehyde
(*b*) A thermosetting plastic
(*c*) Can be used as an adhesive
(*d*) All of the above
Answer. (*d*)
897. Anisole is formed when phenol is treated with
(*a*) $CH_3I/NaOH$
(*b*) $CH_3CH_2I/NaOH$
(*c*) $CHCl_3/NaOH$
(*d*) Acetic anhydride
Answer. (*a*)
898. Anisole on heating with concentrated HI gives
(*a*) Iodobenzene
(*b*) Phenol + CH_3I
(*c*) Iodobenzene + CH_3OH
(*d*) Phenol + CH_3OH
Answer. (*b*)
899. Which group forms the strongest H-bonds to water molecules?
(*a*) Alcohols
(*b*) Ethers
(*c*) Phenols
(*d*) All equally strong
Answer. (*c*)
900. The compound which is most capable of hydrogen bonding is :
(*a*) $CH_3OCH_2CH_3$
(*b*) $CH_3CH_2CH_2CH_3$
(*c*) 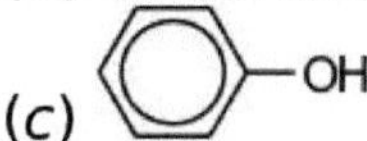

(*d*) $CH_3CH_2—S—S—CH_2CH_3$
Answer. (*c*)
901. Rank the following molecules in decreasing order of boiling points :

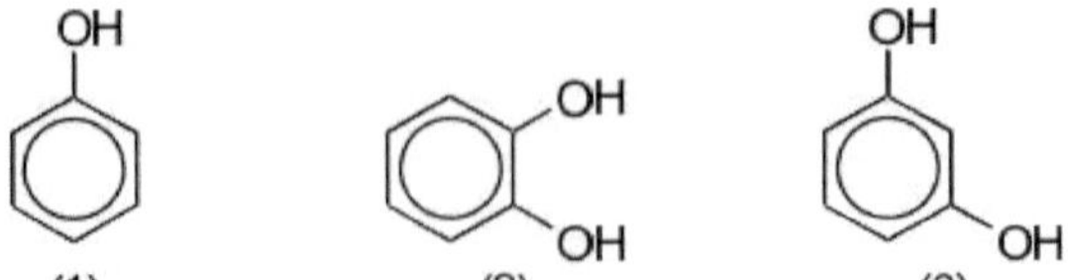

(1) (2) (3)

(*a*) (3) > (2) > (1)
(*b*) (2) > (3) > (1)
(*c*) (3) > (1) > (2)
(*d*) (2) > (1) > (3)
Answer. (*a*). Hydroxyl groups can more easily form intramolecular H-bonds in the *ortho* position than in the *meta* or *para* positions. These intramolecular H-bonds decrease boiling point. Therefore, compound (3) has a higher boiling point than compound (2). Compound (2), with two hydroxyl groups, has a still higher boiling point than phenol.

902. Rank the following compounds in order of increasing boiling point :

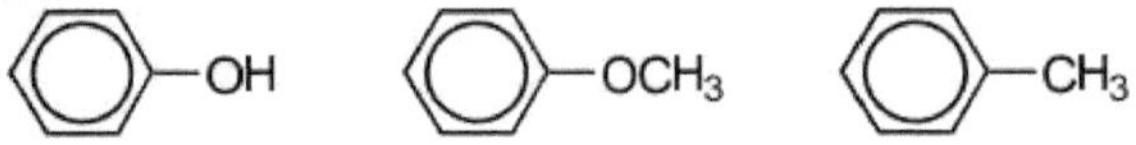

(1) (2) (3)

(*a*) (1) < (2) < (3)
(*b*) (3) < (1) < (2)
(*c*) (1) < (3) < (2)
(*d*) (3) < (2) < (1)
Answer. (*d*)

903. Phenol is acidic because of
(*a*) Resonance
(*b*) Electromeric effect
(*c*) Inductive effect
(*d*) Peroxide effect
Answer. (*a*)

904. Which of the following has the most acidic proton?
(*a*) Thiol
(*b*) Alcohol
(*c*) Phenol

(*d*) Ether
Answer. (*c*)
905. Phenol is
(*a*) stronger acid than acetic acid
(*b*) weaker acid than acetic acid
(*c*) stronger base than methylamine
(*d*) weaker base than methylamine
Answer. (*b*)
906. Which of the following compounds is least acidic?
(*a*) HCl
(*b*) Phenol
(*c*) Acetylene
(*d*) Picric acid
Answer. (*c*)
907. Which of the following compounds is least acidic?
(*a*) Formic acid
(*b*) Ethanol
(*c*) Acetic acid
(*d*) Phenol
Answer. (*b*)
908. Which of the following compounds is most acidic?
(*a*) Formic acid
(*b*) Ethanol
(*c*) Acetic acid
(*d*) Phenol
Answer. (*a*)
909. Which of the following compounds is most acidic?
(*a*) Water
(*b*) Cyclohexanol
(*c*) Ethanol
(*d*) Phenol
Answer. (*d*)
910. Which one is most acidic?
(*a*) Hexanol
(*b*) Phenol
(*c*) Water

(*d*) Diisopropyl ether
Answer. (*b*)
911. Which of the following compounds is most acidic?
(*a*) *o*-Cresol
(*b*) *p*-Nitrophenol
(*c*) *p*-Cresol
(*d*) *p*-Chlorophenol
Answer. (*b*)
912. Which of the following compounds is most acidic?
(*a*) Phenol
(*b*) *m*-Nitrophenol
(*c*) *m*-Cresol
(*d*) *m*-Bromophenol
Answer. (*b*)
913. Which molecule is the most acidic?

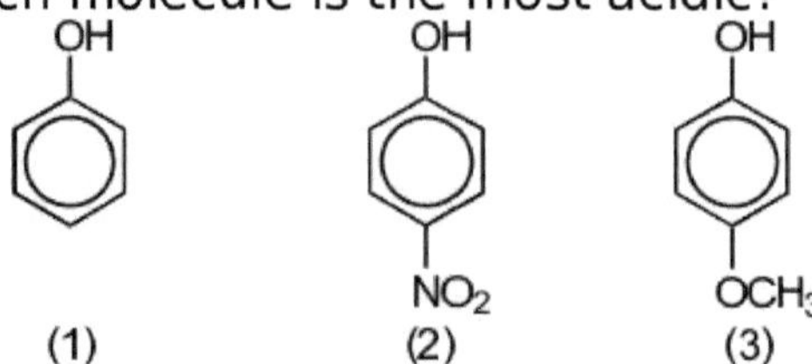

(*a*) (1)
(*b*) (2)
(*c*) (3)
(*d*) (2) and (3) have similar acidities
Answer. (*b*). Acidity is enhanced when the conjugate base is further stabilized. By placing an electron-withdrawing group on the ring, the phenoxide ion is further stabilized when the charge spreads over more atoms (greater delocalization). The methoxy group is electron-releasing and destabilizes the phenoxide.
914. Which of the following compounds is most acidic?

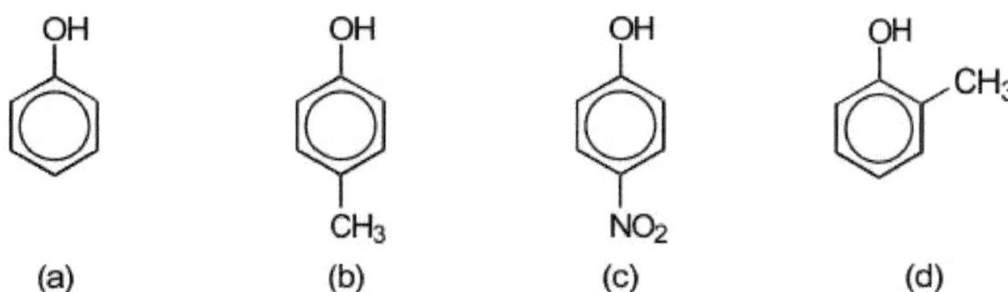

Answer. (*c*)

915. Which of the following compounds is least acidic?

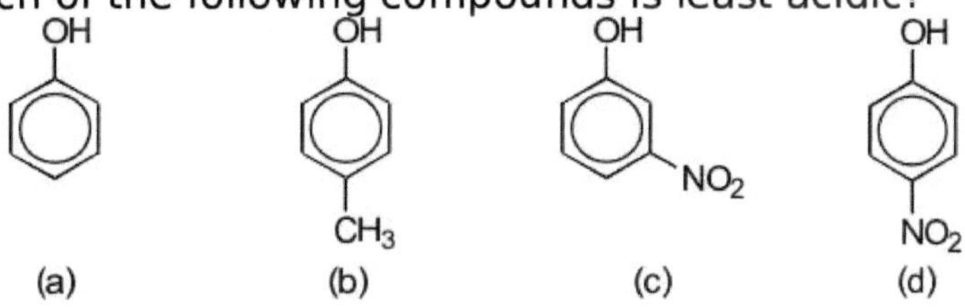

Answer. (*b*)

916. Arrange the following compounds in order of increasing acidity :

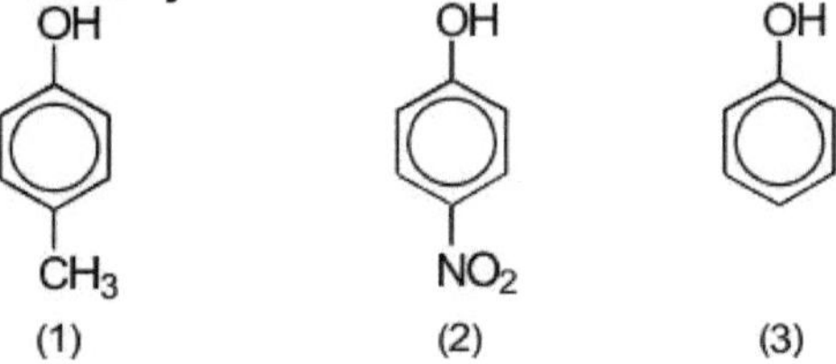

(*a*) (1) < (3) < (2)
(*b*) (1) < (2) < (3)
(*c*) (3) < (2) < (1)
(*d*) (2) < (1) < (3)

Answer. (*a*)

917. Phenols can be easily distinguished from alcohols because

(*a*) phenols are soluble in NaOH, but alcohols are not
(*b*) alcohols are soluble in NaOH, but phenols are not
(*c*) phenols are soluble in $NaHCO_3$, but alcohols are not
(*d*) alcohols are soluble in $NaHCO_3$, but phenols are not

Answer. (*a*)

918. Benzoyl chloride reacts with hydrogen in the presence of palladium and barium sulfate to give :
(*a*) Benzyl alcohol
(*b*) Benzaldehyde
(*c*) Cinnamic acid
(*d*) Benzophenone
Answer. (*b*). This is Rosenmund reduction.
919. Cinnamaldehyde is prepared by the treatment of :
(*a*) benzaldehyde with acetaldehyde in the presence of NaOH
(*b*) benzaldehyde with formaldehyde in the presence of NaOH
(*c*) benzophenone with acetaldehyde in the presence of NaOH
(*d*) benzophenone with formaldehyde in the presence of NaOH
Answer. (*a*)
920. Benzaldehyde reacts with methylmagnesium iodide (followed by hydrolysis) to form
(*a*) 1-Phenylethanol
(*b*) Acetophenone
(*c*) 2-Phenylethanol
(*c*) Benzophenone
Answer. (*a*)
921. Which of the following will undergo Aldol condensation?
(*a*) Acetone
(*b*) Benzaldehyde
(*c*) Benzoic acid
(*c*) Benzophenone
Answer. (*a*)
922. When benzaldehyde is heated with concentrated NaOH, it gives :
(*a*) Benzyl alcohol
(*b*) Sodium benzoate
(*c*) Benzoic acid

(*d*) Benzyl alcohol + Sodium benzoate

Answer. (*d*). This is Cannizzaro reaction.

923. Benzaldehyde reacts with acetic anhydride in the presence of sodium acetate at 180°C to give :

(*a*) Mandelic acid

(*b*) Cinnamic acid

(*c*) Malonic acid

(*d*) Benzoic acid

Answer. (*b*). This is Perkin reaction.

924. Which of the following reagents will give an addition reaction with benzaldehyde?

(*a*) $NaHSO_3$

(*b*) $I_2/NaOH$

(*c*) H_2SO_4

(*d*) $CH_3-\overset{\overset{\displaystyle O}{\|}}{C}-Cl$

Answer. (*a*)

925. Benzaldehyde reacts with a mixture of concentrated sulfuric acid and nitric acid to give

(*a*) *p*-Nitrobenzaldehyde

(*b*) *o*-Nitrobenzaldehyde

(*c*) *p*-Nitrobenzoic acid

(*d*) *m*-Nitrobenzaldehyde

Answer. (*d*)

926. Acetophenone reacts with Br_2 in the presence of $FeCl_3$ to form :

(*a*) *m*-Bromoacetophenone

(*b*) *m*-Dibromobenzene

(*c*) *o*- + *p*-Bromoacetophenone

(*d*) *p*-Dibromobenzene

Answer. (*a*)

927. Which of the following statements is NOT correct :

(*a*) Tollens' test is given by both aliphatic and aromatic aldehydes.

(*b*) Fehling's test is given by aliphatic aldehydes. It is not given by aromatic aldehydes.
(*c*) Iodoform test is given by methyl ketones and acetaldehydes.
(*d*) Lucas test is given by both aliphatic and aromatic aldehydes.
Answer. (*d*)
928. Benzaldehyde can be distinguished from acetophenone by using :
(*a*) Tollens' reagent
(*b*) Lucas reagent
(*c*) Fehling's reagent
(*d*) All of these
Answer. (*a*)
929. Benzaldehyde does not react with
(*a*) Tollens' reagent
(*b*) Phenylhydrazine
(*c*) Fehling's solution
(*d*) $NaHSO_3$
Answer. (*c*)
930. Which of the following will give a positive Tollens' test?
(*a*) $C_6H_5-\overset{\overset{O}{\|}}{C}-C_6H_5$
(*b*) cyclohexanone (ring =O)
(*c*) $CH_3CH_2-\overset{\overset{O}{\|}}{C}-H$
(*d*) cyclohexenone (ring =O)
Answer. (*c*)
931. Which of the following compounds yields a yellow precipitate when warmed with a mixture of iodine in aqueous sodium hydroxide?
(*a*) Acetophenone

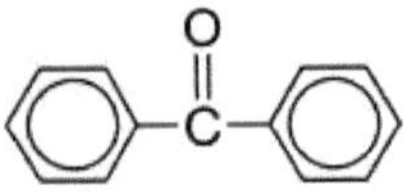

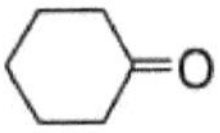

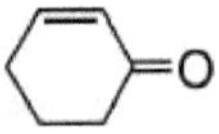

(*b*) Benzaldehyde
(*c*) Benzophenone
(*d*) Propanal
Answer. (*a*)
932. A compound (*A*) gave a positive iodoform reaction and left a solution containing a monocarboxylate ion. Which of the following could (*A*) be?
(*a*) $CH_3-C_6H_4-\overset{O}{\overset{\|}{C}}-H$
(*b*) $C_6H_5-\overset{O}{\overset{\|}{C}}-H$
(*c*) $C_6H_5-\overset{O}{\overset{\|}{C}}-CH_3$
(*d*) $C_6H_5-\overset{O}{\overset{\|}{C}}-CH_2CH_3$
Answer. (*c*)
933. How many isomers containing a benzene ring correspond to the formula $C_6H_4(COOH)_2$?
(*a*) 1
(*b*) 2
(*c*) 3
(*d*) 4
Answer. (c)
934. Which of the following is not a carboxylic acid?
(*a*) Malonic acid
(*b*) Acetic acid
(*c*) Picric acid
(*d*) Adipic acid
Answer. (*c*)
935. Phenylmagnesium bromide reacts with CO_2 followed by acid-hydrolysis to form :
(*a*) Phenol

(*b*) Benzoic acid
(*c*) Bromobenzene
(*d*) Acetophenone
Answer. (*b*)
936. Benzoic acid and diphenyl ketone are both solids insoluble in water. A mixture of these compounds can be separated if we
(*a*) add the mixture to a solution of NaOH in water, and filter.
(*b*) add the mixture to a solution of HCl in water, and filter.
(*c*) dissolve the mixture in benzene and boil off the benzene.
(*d*) It is impossible to separate a mixture of two solids when both are insoluble in water.
Answer. (*a*)
937. Which of the following reactions does not produce benzene as one of the products?
(*a*) Treating benzenediazonium chloride with H_3PO_2
(*b*) Distilling phenol with zinc dust
(*c*) Fusing sodium benzoate with NaOH
(*d*) Fusing sodium benzenesulfonate with NaOH
Answer. (*d*)
938. Which of the following esters produces butyric acid and phenol on hydrolysis?
(*a*) Phenyl butyrate
(*b*) Butyl benzoate
(*c*) Benzyl propionate
(*d*) Phenyl propionate
Answer. (*a*)
939. Benzoyl chloride on basic-hydrolysis ($NaOH/H_2O$) gives :
(*a*) Benzoic acid
(*b*) Methyl benzoate
(*c*) Sodium benzoate
(*d*) Ethyl benzoate
Answer. (*c*)
940. Sodium benzoate on heating with soda-lime gives :

(*a*) Sodium phenoxide
(*b*) Benzene
(*c*) Benzaldehyde
(*d*) Benzophenone
Answer. (*b*)
941. The product of the following reaction is :

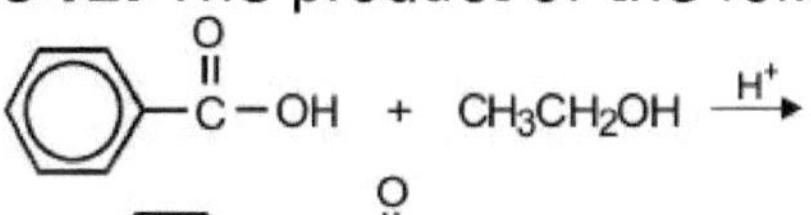

$C_6H_5-\overset{O}{\overset{||}{C}}-OH + CH_3CH_2OH \xrightarrow{H^+}$

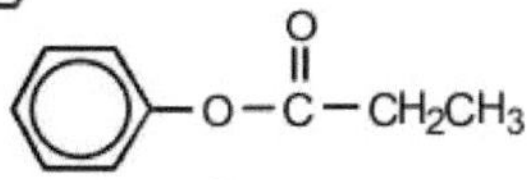

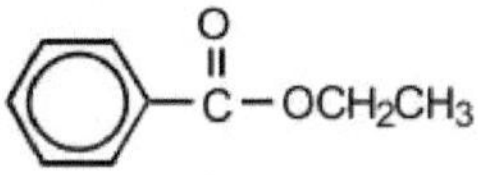

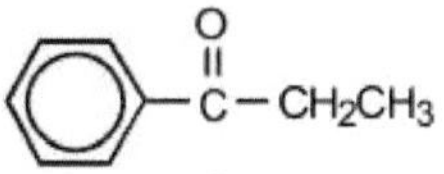

(*a*) $C_6H_5-O-\overset{O}{\overset{||}{C}}-CH_2CH_3$

(*b*) $C_6H_5-\overset{O}{\overset{||}{C}}-OCH_2CH_3$

(*c*) $C_6H_5-\overset{O}{\overset{||}{C}}-CH_2CH_3$

(*d*) $C_6H_5-\overset{O}{\overset{||}{C}}-C_6H_5$

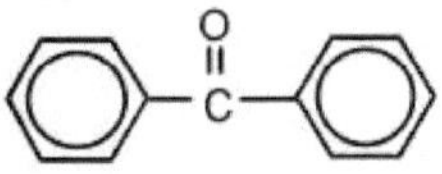

Answer. (*b*)
942. Methyl benzoate on hydrolysis gives
(*a*) Acetic acid
(*b*) Benzoic acid
(*c*) Picric acid
(*d*) Phenylacetic acid
Answer. (*b*)
943. Aspirin is produced by heating salicylic acid with
(*a*) acetic anhydride in the presence of phosphoric acid
(*b*) benzoic anhydride in the presence of phosphoric acid
(*c*) methyl alcohol in the presence of sulfuric acid
(*d*) phenol in the presence of sulfuric acid
Answer. (*a*)
944. Oil of Wintergreen (Methyl salicylate) is obtained by treating salicylic acid with
(*a*) Methane at 150°C
(b) CH_3OH and conc. H_2SO_4

(*c*) Methyl chloride
(d) NaOH and then CH_3OH
Answer. (*b*)
945. Which of the following statements is true :
(*a*) *o*-Nitrobenzoic acid is more acidic than *p*-nitrophenol
(*b*) *o*-Nitrobenzoic acid is less acidic than *p*-nitrophenol
(*c*) *o*-Nitrobenzoic acid and *p*-nitrobenzoic acid have the same acid strength
(*d*) None of these statements is true
Answer. (*a*)
946. The order of increasing acidity is :
(*a*) chloroacetic acid > formic acid > benzoic acid
(*b*) benzoic acid > formic acid > chloroacetic acid
(*c*) all are the same
(*d*) not determinable from available data
Answer. (*a*)
947. Which of the following is the strongest acid?
(*a*) Trichloroacetic acid
(*b*) Phenol
(*c*) Acetic acid
(*d*) Benzoic acid
Answer. (*a*)
948. Which of the following is the strongest acid?
(*a*) Ethanol
(*b*) Phenol
(*c*) Anisole
(*d*) Benzoic acid
Answer. (*d*)
949. Which acid is weaker than benzoic acid?
(*a*) *p*-Methylbenzoic acid
(*b*) *p*-Chlorobenzoic acid
(*c*) *p*-Nitrobenzoic acid
(*d*) *o*-Chlorobenzoic acid
Answer. (*a*)
950. Compound (*A*) when reacted with PCl_5 and then with ammonia gave (*B*). Compound (*B*) when treated with

bromine and NaOH, produced (*C*). Compound (*C*) on treatment with $NaNO_2$/HCl at 0°C and then boiling with H_2O produced o-cresol. Compound (*A*) is
(*a*) *o*-Toluic acid
(*b*) *o*-Chlorotoluene
(*c*) *m*-Toluic acid
(*d*) *o*-Bromotoluene
Answer. (*a*)
951. The reason why materials appear colored is
(*a*) The selective absorption of spectral colors
(*b*) The interaction between the light and the electrons of the dye molecules
(*c*) The composition of the white light from various spectral colors
(*d*) All of these
Answer. (*d*)
952. Which of the following is a chromophore?
(*a*) $-NO_2$
(*b*) $-SO_3H$
(*c*) –OH
(*d*) –COOH
Answer. (*a*)
953. Which of the following is an auxochrome?
(*a*) –N=O
(*b*) $-NO_2$
(*c*) –N=N–
(*d*) –OH
Answer. (*d*)
954. The water-solubility of dyes can be increased by introducing
(*a*) SO_3Na groups
(*b*) COOH groups
(*c*) OH groups
(*d*) All of these
Answer. (*d*)

955. Which dyes become linked to the fibre by chemical reaction?
(*a*) Acid dyes
(*b*) Direct dyes
(*c*) Disperse dyes
(*d*) None of these
Answer. (*a*)
956. All carbon atoms in naphthalene are
(*a*) *sp* hybridized
(*b*) sp^2 hybridized
(*c*) sp^3 hybridized
(*d*) None of these
Answer. (*b*)
957. Naphthalene undergoes oxidation with $Na_2Cr_2O_7$ / H_2SO_4 to form
(*a*) Phthalic acid
(*b*) Phenylacetic acid
(*c*) Tetralin
(*d*) Benzoic acid
Answer. (*a*)
958. Naphthalene undergoes reduction with H_2 in the presence of Ni catalyst at high temperature and pressure to give
(*a*) Phthalic acid
(*b*) Decalin
(*c*) Benzoic acid
(*d*) Tetralin
Answer. (*b*)
959. Naphthalene undergoes nitration with HNO_3/H_2SO_4 at 60°C to give mainly
(*a*) 1-Nitronaphthalene
(*b*) 1,2-Dinitronaphthalene
(*c*) 2-Nitronaphthalene
(*d*) 1,5-Dinitronaphthalene
Answer. (*a*)
960. All carbon atoms in anthracene are

(*a*) *sp* hybridized
(*b*) sp^3 hybridized
(*c*) sp^2 hybridized
(*d*) None of these
Answer. (*c*)
961. Anthracene undergoes electrophilic substitution reactions mainly at
(*a*) C-1
(*b*) C-2
(*c*) C-9
(*d*) C-1 and C-2
Answer. (*c*)
962. Anthracene undergoes oxidation with O_2/V_2O_5 at 500°C to give
(*a*) Benzoic acid
(*b*) Anthraquinone
(*c*) Phthalic acid
(*d*) Benzophenone
Answer. (*b*)
963. Which of the following is not a heterocyclic compound?
(*a*) 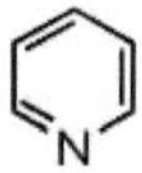 N
(*b*) 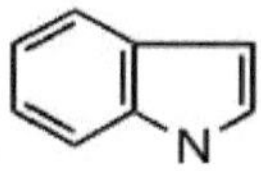 N
(*c*)  O
(*d*)  S
Answer. (*c*)
964. Which of the following heterocyclic compounds is not aromatic?
(*a*) Pyridine
(*b*) Pyrrole

(*c*) Furan
(*d*) Piperidine
Answer. (*d*)
965. The 'N' atom in pyridine is
(*a*) sp^3 hybridized
(*b*) sp^2 hybridized
(*c*) *sp* hybridized
(*d*) cannot be predicted
Answer. (*b*)
966. Pyridine has a delocalized π molecular orbital containing
(*a*) 4 electrons
(*b*) 6 electrons
(*c*) 8 electrons
(*d*) 12 electrons
Answer. (*b*)
967. Pyrrole is less basic than pyridine because the lone-pair of electrons on N-atom in pyrrole
(*a*) is part of the delocalized π molecular orbital.
(*b*) is not part of the delocalized π molecular orbital.
(*c*) resides in sp^2 hybrid orbital
(*d*) resides in *sp* hybrid orbital
Answer. (*a*)
968. Pyridine is less basic than trimethylamine because the lone-pair of electrons on N-atom in pyridine resides in
(*a*) sp^2 hybrid orbital
(*b*) *sp* hybrid orbital
(*c*) sp^3 hybrid orbital
(*d*) *p*-orbital
Answer. (*a*)
969. Pyridine reacts with HCl to form
(*a*) Pyridinium chloride
(*b*) 2-Chloropyridine
(*c*) 3-Chloropyridine
(*d*) All of these
Answer. (*a*)

970. Pyridine undergoes electrophilic substitution with fuming H_2SO_4 at 350°C to give
(*a*) 2-Pyridinesulfonic acid
(*b*) 4-Pyridinesulfonic acid
(*c*) 3-Pyridinesulfonic acid
(*d*) None of these
Answer. (*c*)
971. Pyridine reacts with a mixture of KNO_3 and H_2SO_4 at 300°C to give
(*a*) 1-Nitropyridine
(*b*) 2-Nitropyridine
(*c*) 3-Nitropyridine
(*d*) 4-Nitropyridine
Answer. (*c*)
972. Pyridine undergoes nuclophilic substitution with $NaNH_2$ at 100°C to form
(*a*) 2-Aminopyridine
(*b*) 3-Aminopyridine
(*c*) 4-Aminopyridine
(*d*) None of these
Answer. (*a*)
973. Which of the following reagents will react with pyrrole to form 2-formylpyrrole?
(*a*) HCOOH
(*b*) $CHCl_3$/KOH
(*c*) H_2O_2
(*d*) $(CH_3CO)_2O/SnCl_4$
Answer. (*b*)
974. Furan reacts with ammonia in the presence of alumina at 400°C to give
(*a*) Pyridine
(*b*) Furfural
(*c*) Pyrrole
(*d*) Furoic acid
Answer. (*c*)

975. Which of the following reagents will react with furan to form 2-furansulfonic acid?
(*a*) SO_3 in pyridine at 100°C
(*b*) Dilute H_2SO_4 at 200°C
(*c*) SO_2 at 100°C
(*d*) Dilute H_2SO_4 at 100°C
Answer. (*a*)
976. When aniline is heated with glycerol in the presence of sulfuric acid and nitrobenzene, it gives quinoline. This reaction in called
(*a*) Fischer synthesis
(*b*) Skraup synthesis
(*c*) Diazotization
(*d*) Corey-House synthesis
Answer. (*b*)
977. Quinoline undergoes nucleophilic substitution on heating with $NaNH_2$ to give
(*a*) 2-Aminoquinoline
(*b*) 4-Aminoquinoline
(*c*) 3-Aminoquinoline
(*d*) 8-Aminoquinoline
Answer. (*a*)
978. Orlon is prepared by the polymerisation of
(*a*) Vinyl cyanide
(*b*) Allyl alcohol
(*c*) Vinyl chloride
(*d*) Allyl chloride
Answer. (*a*)
979. Which of the following statements is true about terpenes?
(*a*) They are a class of lipids that can be isolated from plants.
(*b*) They contain carbon atoms in multiples of five.
(*c*) They are composed of isoprene units joined together in a head-to-tail fashion.
(*d*) All of the above

Answer. (*d*)
980. How many isoprene units are in a sesquiterpene?
(*a*) 1
(*b*) 2
(*c*) 3
(*d*) 4
Answer. (*c*)
981. What is the IUPAC name for isoprene?
(*a*) 1,3-pentadiene
(*b*) 2,4-pentadiene
(*c*) 2,3-dimethyl-1, 3-butadiene
(*d*) 2-methyl-1,3-butadiene
Answer. (*d*)
982. How many isoprene units are present in sesquiterpenes?
(*a*) 1
(*b*) 2
(*c*) 3
(*d*) 4
Answer. (*c*)
983. Teflon is prepared by the polymerization of
(*a*) Butadiene
(*b*) Vinyl cyanide
(*c*) Vinyl chloride
(*d*) Tetrafluoroethylene
Answer. (*d*)
984. Bakelite is obtained from :
(*a*) Phenol and formaldehyde
(*b*) Adipic acid and hexamethylene diamine
(*c*) Dimethyl terephthalate and ethylene glycol
(*d*) Neoprene
Answer. (*a*)
985. Nylon-6,6 is obtained from :
(*a*) Adipic acid and hexamethylene diamine
(*b*) Tetrafluoroethylene
(*c*) Vinyl cyanide

(*d*) Vinylbenzene
Answer. (*a*)
986. Neoprene is a polymer of the following monomer
(*a*) Chloroprene
(*b*) Isoprene
(*c*) Isobutane
(*d*) Isopentene
Answer. (*a*)
987. Which of the following is a thermosetting polymer?
(*a*) Bakelite
(*b*) Nylon-6,6
(*c*) Polyethylene
(*d*) Teflon
Answer. (*a*)
988. Which of the following is an example of a condensation polymer?
(*a*) Nylon-6,6
(*b*) Teflon
(*c*) Polypropylene
(*d*) Orlon
Answer. (*a*)
989. Which of the following polymers contain nitrogen
(*a*) PVC
(*b*) Teflon
(*c*) Nylon
(*d*) Terylene
Answer. (*c*)
990. Adipic acid reacts with hexamethylene diamine to form
(*a*) Bakelite
(*b*) Nylon-6,6
(*c*) Terylene
(*d*) Nylon-6,8
Answer. (*b*)
991. Ethylene glycol reacts with dimethyl terephthalate to form
(*a*) Nylon-6,6

(*b*) Teflon
(*c*) Dacron
(*d*) Orlon
Answer. (*c*)
992. Natural rubber is a polymer of
(*a*) Propene
(*b*) Isoprene
(*c*) Formaldehyde
(*d*) Phenol
Answer. (*b*)
993. The monomers for *Buna-S* are 1,3-butadiene and
(*a*) Ethylene glycol
(*b*) Adipic acid
(*c*) Styrene
(*d*) Caprolactum
Answer. (*c*)
994. Which of the following statements is *not* true?
(*a*) Natural rubber is a hydrocarbon.
(*b*) Natural rubber is made of isoprene units
(*c*) Natural rubber is a polymer of 1,3-Butadiene
(*d*) Natural rubber can be vulcanized.
Answer. (*c*)
995. Which of the following are addition polymers?
I. Polypropylene
II. Teflon
III. Nylon
(*a*) Only I
(*b*) Only II
(*c*) Only III
(*d*) both I and II
Answer. (*d*)
996. Which of the following are condensation polymers?
I. Polypropylene
II. Teflon
III. Nylon
(*a*) Only I

(*b*) Only II
(*c*) Only III
(*d*) Both II and III
Answer. (*c*)
997. Which one of the following is used to make Teflon?
(*a*) Fluoroethene
(*b*) 1,1,4,4-tetrafluorobutadiene
(*c*) 1,2-difluoroethene
(*d*) Tetrafluoroethylene
Answer. (*d*)
998. Vulcanization is the process of cross-linking polymer chains in rubber using
(*a*) Sulfur.
(*b*) Formaldehye.
(*c*) Benzoyl peroxide.
(*d*) Ethylene glycol.
Answer. (*a*)
999. What is the purpose of plasticizers?
(*a*) Harden plastics
(*b*) Soften plastics
(*c*) Initiate polymerizations
(*d*) Cross-link polymer chains
Answer. (*b*)
1000. Polymers which soften on heating and harden when cooled are
(*a*) Cross-linked polymers
(*b*) Copolymers
(*c*) Thermosetting polymers
(*d*) Thermoplastics
Answer. (*d*)

9 798885 037648

Printed by Libri Plureos GmbH in Hamburg,
Germany